Dungeon Hacks

Dungeon Hacks

How NetHack, Angband, and Other Roguelikes
Changed the Course of Video Games

David L. Craddock

CRC Press
Taylor & Francis Group
Boca Raton London New York

CRC Press is an imprint of the
Taylor & Francis Group, an **informa** business

First Edition published 2022
by CRC Press
6000 Broken Sound Parkway NW, Suite 300, Boca Raton, FL 33487-2742

and by CRC Press
2 Park Square, Milton Park, Abingdon, Oxon, OX14 4RN

CRC Press is an imprint of Taylor & Francis Group, LLC

ISBN: 978-1-032-05240-3 (hbk)
ISBN: 978-1-032-05154-3 (pbk)
ISBN: 978-1-003-19671-6 (ebk)

Typeset in Adobe Garamond Pro
by Straive, India

Books by David L. Craddock

Fiction

Arthur and the Knights of the Cafeteria Table (2021)

The Dumpster Club

Heritage: Book One of the Gairden Chronicles

Point of Fate: Book Two of the Gairden Chronicles

Firebug: War of the Elementalists

Nonfiction

Stay Awhile and Listen: Book I – How Two Blizzards Unleashed Diablo and Forged a Video-Game Empire

Stay Awhile and Listen: Book II – Heaven, Hell, and Secret Cow Levels

Arcade Perfect: How Pac-Man, Mortal Kombat, and Other Coin-Op Classics Invaded the Living Room

Monsters in the Dark: The Making of X-COM: UFO Defense

Beneath a Starless Sky: Pillars of Eternity and the Infinity Engine Era of RPGs

Rocket Jump: Quake and the Golden Age of First-Person Shooters

Break Out: How the Apple II Launched the PC Gaming Revolution

Dungeon Hacks: How NetHack, Angband, and Other Roguelikes Changed the Course of Video Games

Shovel Knight (Boss Fight Books)

Bottomless Pit: Bottomless Pit: Running and Jumping Through Platform Games - Volume 1

GameDev Stories: Interviews About Game Development and Culture

GameDev Stories: Volume 2 – More Interviews About Game Development and Culture

Once Upon a Point and Click: The Tale of King's Quest, Gabriel Knight, and the Queens of Adventure Games

One-Week Dungeons: Diaries of a Seven-Day Roguelike Challenge

Making Fun: Stories of Game Development - Volume 1

Angels, Devils, and Boomsticks: The Making of Demons with Shotguns

Anything But Sports: The Making of FTL

Red to Black: The Making of Rogue Legacy

Everybody Shake! The Making of Spaceteam

Stairway to Badass: The Making and Remaking of Doom (TBD 2021)

Ascendant: The Fall of Tomb Raider and the Rise of Lara Croft (TBD 2021)

Bet on Black: How Microsoft and the Xbox Changed Pop Culture (TBD 2022)

Better Together: Stories of EverQuest (TBD)

Table of Contents

About This Book

Dungeon Hacks consists of three primary sections: the Main Book, Side Quests, and Bonus Rounds.

Main Book

Dungeon Hacks comprises ten chapters. You can skip the Side Quests and Bonus Rounds if you like, but you'll miss out on lots of behind-the-scenes stories and information if you do.

Side Quests

Side Quests collect bonus material. At the end of select chapters, you'll find Side Quests related to content discussed in the chapter. You can read them, or skip ahead to the next chapter and save the Side Quests for later.

Bonus Rounds

Bonus Rounds are extra chapters that expand on people, events, and games related to the Main Book. You can read the Bonus Rounds whenever you choose, but they are best absorbed after finishing the Main Book.

Introduction: Rodney and Friends

Ancient Domains of Mystery (*ADOM*) is the newest roguelike role-playing game you'll read about in *Dungeon Hacks*, and it's over twenty years old. The oldest of the bunch is nearing forty. "So what's the point?" I hear you ask. "Just what is a roguelike? What's this book all about? And who is Rodney, anyway?"

You'll meet Rodney in due time. Meanwhile, allow me to answer your other questions.

Although the definition of "roguelike" is up in the air, the gist of it is a game featuring tactical play, procedurally generated levels, and permanent death. "Tactical play" usually means "turn by turn," like chess. "Procedurally generated" means "built by following an algorithm," causing levels to be baked from scratch every time you play. Permanent death should be obvious: One life, one chance. Die, and you start over from the beginning.

The oldest roguelike games featured primitive graphics. Instead of pixels and polygons, these primordial creations are displayed using text: capital letters for monsters, special symbols like "!" and "#" for treasures, items, and architecture, and the "@" sign for little old you. And here's the kicker: in many ways, those text characters were more evocative than the slickest, most modern graphics engine on the market today.

Dungeon Hacks is a story about people. While I've devoted plenty of pages to discussion of design, I focused on the founders of the roguelike genre: who they are, where they came from in terms of motivations and influences, and how their backgrounds and the culture of the day informed their creations. By reading *Dungeon Hacks*, you'll gain an understanding and appreciation for how they influenced other game developers down the line. Some of those developers probably went on to create some of your favorite games, and you've got roguelikes to thank for them.

Determining which games to cover in the book was tough...and yet simple, too. I knew I couldn't write a book about roguelikes without covering *Rogue*, and *NetHack* and *Angband* are arguably as popular today as they were twenty years ago.

In order to keep the book's scope manageable, I had to let some games go. You'll find no mention of *Dungeon Crawl Stone Soup*, *Larn*, *Brogue*, *Tales of Maj'Eyal* (*TOME*), or others within this TOME because they fell outside the eras I decided to concentrate on and/or because another game came along first and set the mold in which they were baked.

The omission of these games does not indicate a lack of importance on their part or due diligence on mine. The book's dance card was full, that's all.

Roguelikes may never be a mainstream, big-budget genre able to go toe to toe with *Call of Duty* on sales chart, but they don't have to be. Browse the Steam storefront and you'll peruse hundreds of roguelikes, as well as roguelike-likes, games influenced by *Rogue* and its offspring.

By the end of *Dungeon Hacks*, I think you'll agree that the roguelike genre's contributions to virtually every type of game you enjoy are undeniable. There are many people to thank for that, and I'm excited for you to meet a few of them.

- David L. Craddock

Acknowledgments

To the forebears of the roguelike genre: Thank you for letting me pick your brains.
To Andrew: Thank you for your friendship and keen eye.
To Mom and Amie: Thank you for your love and support.

About the Author

David L. Craddock lives with his wife, Amie Kline-Craddock, in Canton, Ohio. He is the author of several books including *Stay Awhile and Listen: Book I—How Two Blizzards Unleashed Diablo and Forged a Video-Game Empire*, and *Heritage: Book One of the Gairden Chronicles*. Follow David online at davidlcraddock.com, facebook.com/davidlcraddock, and @davidlcraddock on Twitter.

The BAM-Like
Exploring Beneath Apple Manor

Beneath Apple Manor. Colored blocks represent in-game actors like monsters, treasure, and the player. Here, the player encounters a slime standing near a treasure chest. Blocks between each room represent doors. (Image: CRPG Addict.)

Environmental Conditions

In biology, convergent evolution is the process by which unrelated organisms develop similar traits as a result of adapting to similar environmental conditions. Convergent evolution occurs frequently in nature. Bats, birds, insects, and pterosaurs all developed wings because they were forced to acclimatize to similar environments, even though none of the species are closely related.

Convergent evolution has been known to occur in video games as well.

Rogue is popularly credited as the progenitor of the roguelike, a subgenre of computer role-playing games (CRPGs) known for procedurally generated levels, turn-based gameplay, items bearing randomly assigned properties, and irreversible death. While the genre bears its name, *Rogue* was not the first of its kind. Don Worth got there first.

Worth discovered computers when he enrolled at University of California San Diego as an undergrad in 1967. He became entranced by the colossal mainframes that took up whole rooms and stored data on punch cards instead of hard drives. One of his first pet projects was learning DITRAN (Diagnostic FORmula TRANslating System), a programming language created for the express purpose of crunching advanced physics computations.

In 1968, Worth transferred to University of California Los Angeles (UCLA) and got a job in the university's computer center, then known as Campus Computing Network. His job was to write software in assembly language that ran on the university's IBM System 360, a mainframe connected to the Department of Defense's Advanced Research Projects Agency Network (ARPANET). Heralded as the precursor to the Internet, ARPANET was built so scientists and military personnel could share information. The growing web of connected mainframes included most University of California campuses, and Worth's code facilitated communication between UCLA and other mainframes on the network.

As one of the first individuals to explore cyberspace while its virtual galaxies were still forming, Worth put his programming skills and network access to good use. "A couple of us had written a space game called *FRON* on the mainframe," he told me.[1]

> You'd enter in moves for your ships, and then overnight, there'd be a turnover, and you'd get back a map of all the ship movements and figure out what you were going to do for the next move. It was all partial information—meaning, the computer knew where all the ships were, but you only knew where your ships were and maybe [you knew the contents of] a square or two around them.

Outside the computer lab and away from their homemade space-faring game, Worth and his buddies played *Dungeons & Dragons*. They immersed themselves in the fantasy of exploring strange places, unearthing fantastic treasures, and rolling dice to determine whether their intrepid party of programmers-turned-adventurers lived or perished.

In 1978, Worth and a friend split the cost of an Apple II computer. Hashing out a deal analogous to a custody agreement, Worth got to keep the computer for two weeks before turning it over to his friend for another fortnight. Worth spent his computing time learning Integer BASIC, a language crafted by Apple engineer Steve Wozniak and a staple available on all Apple II machines. Naturally, his inclination was to write a computer simulation of *Dungeons & Dragons*.

BAM

The concept Worth laid out for his game was simple. Players would create an adventurer and explore dungeons inhabited by fearsome creatures that guarded magical artifacts. In RPG parlance, the game would be a dungeon hack, an adventure focused purely on fighting and plundering.

Like his space game, Worth's dungeon hack forced adventurers to go into new environments blind. Players started on a single square. Only adjacent squares were viewable; the rest of the dungeon was cloaked in darkness. Step by step, the darkness peeled back to uncover chambers and winding passageways. The goal of the game was to delve deep beneath stately Apple Manor and recover the fabled golden apple. Worth called his game *Beneath Apple Manor*, or *BAM* for short. "I figured since I was writing it for the Apple, I needed to have 'Apple' in the name, and then I just invented the back-story about a manor house with a dungeon under it."

In the initial, low-resolution version of *Beneath Apple Manor*, color-coding game elements gave the illusion of movement. All floor tiles were gray, and a blue square represented the player-character. When the player pressed the N, S, E, or W keys to move in a cardinal direction, Worth lit the adjacent square blue to show the player's new location, and painted his previous location floor-tile gray.

With the premise set, Worth began adding meat to *Beneath Apple Manor*'s bones. He imported abilities and rules that he and his friends employed in their *D&D* campaigns—listening at doors to detect noise and movement within, breaking down a door, and casting an x-ray spell to reveal the level map. Play proceeded according to turns: first players moved, and then the monsters took a turn, and so on, affording players limitless time to mull over each action.

Worth also tried his hand at writing algorithms that drew brand new levels every time players sat down to the game. To Worth and his friends, part of the fun of *Dungeons & Dragons* was coming across strange new places. They never knew what dangers might lie in wait around the next turn, which blanketed *BAM* in suspense and trepidation. One cocksure or poorly calculated move and their avatars could be killed off.

One of Worth's references for generating levels was *Dragon Maze*, an Apple II game that drew random mazes.

> I set the dimensions, the X and Y coordinates of the far corners [of the level], and just plopped them randomly on the screen. So rooms tended to overlap sometimes or sit right next to each other. I kind of copied *Dragon Maze* and had the program do a random walk from the upper-left hand corner of a room until it hit open space in another room. Those turns were the corridors connecting each room to the others. I had to write some code to make sure I didn't have a room sitting out by itself someplace.

Once a level was generated, Worth populated it with colored blocks representing doors (brown), a single treasure (yellow), and monsters. The strength of the monsters roaming each level depended on how deep beneath the manor players had descended, as well as their experience level. Like the game's rules, its bestiary came from *D&D*: green slimes, purple worms, ghosts, trolls, and dragons.

Each player-character started with strength, intelligence, dexterity, and body, an attribute that represented health. In *D&D*, higher stats equaled greater strength. *BAM* treated stats like pools. Bashing doors and monsters drained strength, casting spells lowered intelligence, moving exhausted dexterity, and taking damage lowered body. In effect, players grew fatigued from performing actions. Standing still slowly refilled each attribute, which added to tension: players could find a hiding spot from monsters when their stats ran low. Despite the risk of exhaustion, players were encouraged to kill monsters to earn experience points. At the end of each level, they could trade experience points to deepen their pools of stats, and spend gold on weapons.

Slaying monsters was easier said than done. Bumping into a monster initiated an attack and gave monsters the chance to retaliate. Higher stats translated to greater accuracy in battle;

many low-level monsters missed much more often than they hit, but players could suffer the same misfortune. If a monster gained the upper hand, players could break away and attempt to regroup.

Monster vulnerabilities and level layout added other layers of strategy. Doors automatically locked behind players after they passed through thresholds, allowing players to barricade themselves inside rooms simply by walking through the doorway. Many level layouts included secret passageways that players could find by bashing walls or casting the x-ray spell.

Worth coded ingenious workarounds that flew in the face of the Apple II's hardware limitations.

> Originally, I wrote it all in BASIC, and it was just too slow to update the screen, so I wrote an assembler language subroutine to do screen updates. Also, I wanted sounds. I had the *Apple Talker* product and had recorded a couple of sounds: door bash, sword clash. Then I reverse-engineered the playback part of *Apple Talker* and rewrote it in assembler [to speed up processing].

All of Worth's solutions were born of improvisation. The door-bash sound came from him thumping his fist on the table near his recorder.[2] For the sound of a successful hit with a sword, he clinked a fork against a glass. Without a printer to generate backup listings of the game's code, he hand-wrote the program in pencil on a yellow legal pad, erasing lines when he needed to make modifications and squeezing in new lines when ideas came to him.

His design-as-you-go approach gave rise to stratagems in *BAM* that continue to prevail in contemporary roguelike games. A few times a week, his friends would come over and put *BAM* through its paces. When they exposed unintended tactics, such as charging through a level to grab the treasure without engaging any monsters, Worth weighed the pros and cons of leaving the strategy intact. More often than not, he decided in favor of the player.

> Generally speaking, the constraints in the game, such as the arrays dictating how many monsters I can have on the screen simultaneously, are going to exist. As a player, if you know what the limits are, you can create strategies based on [those constraints].

Worth loved the idea of skirting around monsters to stock up on magical objects.

> I remember writing in the manual that one of the tricks that could be done was to try and get as many of the magic items as possible first, so you would have an advantage over the monsters. There's one magic item on each level located in a random treasure chest. I even revealed in the manual that it was, generally speaking, a treasure chest in the most upper-left part of the screen.

Stockpiling items early came with another advantage. Each game session generated only one of each magical item. Players were rewarded for finding key items early, such as the boots of silence that muted their footsteps, and the potion of clairvoyance that revealed the map for every level as soon as players set foot in it.

Invariably, players would meet their demise at the hands of one of *BAM*'s denizens. Dying in *BAM* shaved a few points from each attribute, but let players continue their quest. Worth wanted another option, a method of resurrection that players could factor into their strategy for winning the game. His solution was the brain scan. For a price, players could scan their characters, a process that saved their stats, gold, and inventory. Upon resurrection, characters reverted to the state of their last scan.

Worth and his friends had invented the brain scan spell while playing *D&D*, which featured no default method of raising fallen avatars. They hated the fact that when their characters died, they were gone for good. Hours spent working together, leveling up their skills, and stuffing packs full of wealth and baubles—all stolen by an unlucky roll of the dice. In *D&D* and in *BAM*, brain scan kept the fun going as long as possible, but at a cost. Each subsequent scan cost more gold, forcing players to think hard over when to save their progress and when to risk pushing deeper into uncharted territory.

Going Commercial

Worth and his friends deemed *BAM* a good game. Good enough, they thought, to sell it in stores. Partnering with the buddy who had gone fifty-fifty with him on the Apple II, and bringing in another friend, Worth formed The Software Factory in 1978, the same year he wrote *Beneath Apple Manor*. While Worth finished up *BAM*, his other friends wrote more software including tic-tac-toe games and *AppleAstro*, an astrology application. Family pitched in when needed.

> I had my mother-in-law putting packages together. She'd assemble and bind the manuals and stuff the Ziploc baggies for me, and then I'd go out with a boxful of them and visit every computer store in the L.A. area where I lived. I'd say, 'Hey, here's a free computer game. Try it out. If you want to stock it, let me know.'

In 1978, the Apple II's library of games was pitifully low. The dearth of entertainment software paid off for Worth. He caught wind of kids wandering into software stores and getting hooked on copies of *BAM* running on store computers. Despite its relative popularity, the game didn't take off. Sales initially flooded in, then dwindled to a trickle. Worth and his business partners kept their day jobs and spent their nights packaging and shipping software, but the long hours wore thin.

Worth eventually turned to another interest. A friend was writing a comprehensive manual for the Exidy Sorcerer computer to be published by Quality Software. Worth's friend advised him to pay the publisher a visit. On his friend's advice, he went to Quality Software and received a generous offer. Quality Software took charge of marketing *Beneath Apple Manor*, while Worth programmed high-resolution versions of the game for Apple II and PC over 1982 and 1983. Gray squares were replaced by tiles that resembled cobblestone. The blue square that had represented the player-character was swapped out in favor of a tiny warrior carrying a sword and shield. Monsters were likewise given a graphical makeover. Boasting other technical advantages, *Beneath Apple Manor: Special Edition* shipped on a diskette, whereas the original had come on a cassette tape.

After putting the finishing touches on *Beneath Apple Manor* for PC, Worth let his first love, exploring computers, subsume his interest in writing games. The same friend who had published a book through Quality Software got together with Worth and dissected an Apple II disk drive. Placing the drive on Worth's kitchen table, they removed the chassis, slipped in a disk, and watched, mesmerized, as the drive's arm waved back and forth, summoning data from different sectors on the disk like a magician performing a trick with a flourish.

Worth[3] continued probing and eventually reverse engineered Apple DOS, the operating system (OS) that managed the computer's hardware functions. Studying the OS's inner workings, he came across all sorts of subroutines that let users perform operations—none of which had been documented. He spelled them out in *Beneath Apple DOS*.

"I wanted to write and publish *Beneath Apple DOS* so other people could take advantage of the capability that was hidden in the operating system," Worth said. "I guess I decided I would rather write the book than continue developing games. As it turned out, we sold way more copies of *Beneath Apple DOS* than *Beneath Apple Manor*."

Several years passed. Worth entertained the notion of writing a new *BAM* set in a vast wilderness instead of musty dungeons, but the idea fell by the wayside. *BAM* withered and eventually disappeared from Worth's archives. When roguelike communities sprang up on the Internet, *BAM* experienced a surge of renewed interest.

> Somebody contacted me and said, 'Do you have a working copy of the game?' I said, 'No. Actually, I only have a copy-protected, commercial copy of the game.' He said, 'Is it okay if I crack it?' And I said, 'Sure. But please put it in the public domain.'

Great-Grandfathers

While few gamers remember *Beneath Apple Manor*, its influence should not go overlooked. Worth published the first edition of his game in 1978, years before *Rogue* spread across college computer labs. The proliferation of *Rogue* was directly responsible for the genre adopting its namesake rather than that of *BAM*, a game released on a home computer that most users never took online.

Still other species of what are popularly known as roguelikes exhibited features similar to *BAM*, but ahead of Worth's creation. *Dungeon*, written sometime in 1975 or 1976 by Don Daglow, was conceived as a digital version of *Dungeons & Dragons*, then a new game. Its levels were rendered using text characters, and players controlled a party of adventurers instead of a single hero. Around the same time, Ray Wood and Gary Whisenhunt created *DND*, another *Dungeons & Dragons*-like where players ventured through a series of mazes in search of treasure. Another programmer, Daniel Lawrence, wrote a dungeon-maze game called *Telengard* in 1978.

Nevertheless, *Beneath Apple Manor* holds the honor of being the first CRPG released commercially.[3] "At some point, it was years since I had made any money on the game, and so I really don't care about that anymore," Worth said.

> It's just fun to know that people still have fun with it. I hear from players every once in a while, and it always makes me feel good to hear, 'When I was growing up, this was the game I played on my grandpa's Apple II.'

Conversely, *Rogue* started out as a free game, a decision that would both help and hurt its status as the community-appointed grandfather of the genre.

*   *   *

Side Quests

(Turn to page 11 for Chapter 2)

All in the Family

Don Worth brought friends and family into the *Beneath Apple Manor* fold. His brother, Steve, was 11 years younger than Don, and an art major at UCLA during the time Don was developing *BAM*. "He did all the illustrations for the original version of *Beneath Apple Manor*," Worth confirmed, pleased that Steve could illustrate the monsters that the Apple II's limited hardware represented only as colored blocks or text characters.

The siblings bonded over *Dungeons & Dragons* as well. Every night, Don guided Steve and his friends as the group's Dungeon Master.

> I remember thinking it was kind of interesting that the people I was used to playing with at UCLA, all the programmers, were really careful when they'd go into a room. They'd scout it out and try to take it without any blood loss on their part. Steve and his friends, on the other hand, would charge in willy nilly and lots of them got killed because I had scaled the room to be a challenge for the UCLA folks.

As a result of Steve's party's kill-or-be-killed play style, resurrections were cast nearly as often as fireballs.

> There were all these resurrections going on, and I just thought it was fun. They enjoyed the game so much, and all the side effects they were experiencing from resurrecting were a hoot. It opened my eyes to a different play style.

Beyond *BAM*

Like many roguelike authors, Worth entertained notions of taking his dungeon-crawler out of musty cells and into the wilderness. "About the time the Macintosh came out, I got [an Apple] Lisa. Paid $10,000 for it; I have never paid that much for a computer before or since!" he recalled. The Lisa, named after Apple co-founder Steve Jobs' daughter, sported advanced hardware such as support for as much as 2 megabytes (MB) of memory, an operating system that ran on a hard disk, and a graphical user interface (GUI).

Worth hoped to wring every last drop of performance out of the Lisa's hardware with his *BAM* sequel.

> The concept I wanted to follow was something I read in an ACM SIG Graph journal. It dealt with Boeing's use of fractal mathematics to construct random geography, such as land masses, for flight simulators. So I came up with some code in the Pascal language that would generate random surfaces, world surfaces.

Using his code, Worth could input any X/Y coordinates and let the program generate world geography on the fly. His early programs created sample geography with visible oceans and mountaintops. Soon enough, the scope of his ideas stalled the project.

I started making a list of all the things I wanted to do in the game, and the list got longer and longer. I was pretty busy with writing my book, *Beneath Apple DOS*, at the time, and the outdoor *Beneath Apple Manor* project sort of bogged down under its own weight.

R&D

Worth did not peddle *Beneath Apple Manor* arbitrarily. Paging through issues of magazines, he and his friends made a list of the stores that advertised in the pages of *BYTE!*, *Creative Computing*, and other popular periodicals.

> Then we shipped them a three-ring binder with all the manuals for all our software, and a set of disks, and just said, 'If you like this, here's how you can order it.' That worked really well. We were getting orders from all over the place. Downers Grove in Illinois was a really big customer for us, I remember. There must be more copies of *Beneath Apple Manor* in Illinois than any other place.

Options

Both the original and special edition versions of *Beneath Apple Manor* strived to cater to as many users as possible. In the original version, players could choose between "lo-res" graphics, where the player, monsters, and other elements were represented by colored blocks; or a text-only mode that represented elements using letters and symbols. The special edition retained the text-only mode for users without color monitors, and replaced lo-res options with the "hi-res" images.

Roguelikes and BAM-Likes

Beneath Apple Manor pre-dated *Rogue*, yet the genre bears the roguelike name. The moniker's credit likely has to do with *Rogue*'s free and widespread availability in comparison to *BAM*'s status as a commercial product that disappeared from catalogs and stores rather quickly.

Worth, who had never played *Rogue* before developing *BAM*, agreed.

> I'm not that familiar with *Rogue* history, but I think it started out on mainframes over the ARPANET. So I think more people got exposed to it, at least people at universities that were connected to ARPANET. Then it started getting ported to lots of platforms, and I assume it got ported to more platforms than just Apple and PC, as *Beneath Apple Manor* was. It was also a bigger and more elaborate implementation. *Beneath Apple Manor* was small and its playability was highly distilled.

Beneath Apple Archives

Worth gathered up all of his notes, game code, and books and sent them to an Apple II historian. The contents included the folder that contained his handwritten code listings for *Beneath Apple Manor*; the original ink drawings his brother, Steve Worth, illustrated for the game's instruction manual; editions of *Beneath Apple DOS* and *Beneath Apple ProDOS* in paperback, both published by Quality Software; and several software applications on which Worth was the principal programmer or, as in the case of *Ali Baba*, a contributor.

> For *Beneath Apple Manor Special Edition*, I reverse engineered the 6502 runtime environment for the Galfo Integer BASIC compiler and ported it to 8086 machines (IBM PC). Bob Christiansen of Quality Software also ported it to the Atari. I did not write *Ali Baba*— Bob might have—but it was in integer BASIC too I think, so Quality used the Galfo compiler on it to port it between machines too. Bob must have given me a copy, which is why I had it.

Lineage

Naming *Beneath Apple Manor* as the first commercially available CRPG was a big claim, and a difficult one to prove. The Apple II was released in 1977, making it one of the first widely available and affordable microcomputers alongside the Commodore PET and Tandy TRS-80. Prior to their availability, users either used programs distributed part and parcel with operating systems like UNIX, or wrote their own. It stood to reason, then, that *BAM*'s release in 1978 was at least one of the first commercial CRPGs, if not *the* first.

Wanting definitive proof, I contacted Chester Bolingbroke, an RPG enthusiast who has made it his mission to play through four decades' worth of CRPGs, and the maintainer of *CRPG Addict*, the blog where I found *BAM* listed as the first commercially available CRPG. "In all my investigations, I've been unable to track down a commercial RPG released earlier than 1978," Bolingbroke wrote to me. "MobyGames, one of the most comprehensive sources on the Internet, gives 1978 as the first year of any commercial RPG, as does Wikipedia. In almost five years of blogging, no one has come forward with an earlier title."

Two other titles with RPG elements were released around the same time as *BAM*, but *BAM* still seems the most likely candidate. Sources vary on whether *Space*, a deeply involving text-only game, came out in 1978 or 1979. *Dungeon Campaign* was a party-based game where the player controlled a band of characters through a series of levels, and was published by Synergistic Software in December 1978 according to a comment made by Synergistic founder Robert Clardy on *CRPG Addict*'s review of the game.[4] Worth recalls showing off *BAM* in computer stores during autumn of 1978.

Notes

1. A couple of us had written a space game: Interview with Don Worth. All quotes from Don Worth come from interviews conducted via phone and email over 2012–2014.
2. All of Worth's solutions were born of improvisation: "Gallery of Undiscovered Entities." *CGW Museum*. http://gue.cgwmuseum.org/galleries/index.php?pub=0&item=14&id=2&key=0.
3. The first CRPG released commercially: "Game 79: Beneath Apple Manor (1978)." *The CRPG Addict*. http://crpgaddict.blogspot.com/2012/12/game-79-beneath-apple-manor-1978.html.
4. According to a comment made by Synergistic founder Robert Clardy: "Game 83: Dungeon Campaign: 1978." *The CRPG Addict*. http://crpgaddict.blogspot.com/2013/01/game-83-dungeon-campaign-1979.html.

2

Procedural Dungeons of Doom
Building Rogue, *Part 1*

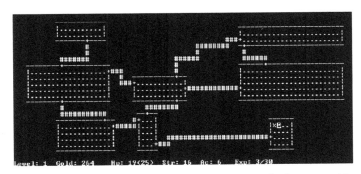

Rogue. The player, represented by the "@" sign, approaches the staircase to the next level, represented by the percent "%" sign. (Image: Wikipedia.)

A Thirst for Adventure

Michael Toy was well aware that computers were good for things besides playing games. He just didn't care. "I grew up in Livermore, California, and in Livermore, you were either a nuclear physicist or a cowboy. My dad was the nuclear physicist type."[1]

His father's credentials came with privileges. One day a year, families were allowed to visit the laboratory. The scientists spared no expense to make the annual visitor's day a memorable outing. Part of the appeal for Toy was getting to operate the facility's mainframe, which was repurposed as a gaming machine for the special occasion.

The flagship title in the lab's modest library of games was *Star Trek*, an adventure that consisted purely of text output. Players controlled the Enterprise, represented by an "-E-", and maneuvered the famous ship around an eight-by-eight quadrant of dots. The goal was to hunt down Klingon ships, represented by "+K+". A readout informed players of their remaining weapons, the health of the Enterprise, and number of Klingons still lurking in the area. *Star Trek* required players to think before they acted. Every action drained energy from the Enterprise, but certain actions revealed information that helped players concoct energy-efficient plans of attack. For example, performing long- and short-range scans of the quadrant uncovered the locations of stars and enemy ships.

Star Trek's depth spurred Toy to try his hand at programming games. "I wrote a clone of that game for every new computer system I encountered for the next 15 years." Thanks to his father's work, he got the opportunity to write and play computer games at home. In the late 1970s, Processor Technology Corporation released the Sol-20 microcomputer, which ran at 2 megahertz and came with a built-in video card that could connect to color-graphics monitors, a novelty for personal computers of the time. Toy wrote *Star Trek* and other games on the Sol-20; his passion grew when he acquired an Atari 400 and other computers later on.

Toy's love of computers and games reached new heights when he enrolled in college in the late 1970s. "I was theoretically attending [University of California] Santa Cruz at the time I started working on *Rogue*. Meaning, I was enrolled, but I was never anywhere except in the computer lab." UC Santa Cruz had all the latest machines including a PDP-11/70, a minicomputer—one size smaller than a mainframe, but a size larger than a microcomputer, also known as a desktop—made by Digital Equipment Corporation as wide as a bookshelf and covered in vents, blinking lights, and large controls that looked like oversized light switches.

Toy didn't get much face time with the 11/70; the massive machine was stored in a basement, flickering away in the darkness. Users in the computer lab connected to the minicomputer through a dumb terminal—a monitor and a keyboard housed in a plastic shell. Dumb terminals had no processing abilities of their own. Instead, they served as translators. Users sent commands to minicomputers or mainframes through the terminal's keyboard, and the computer sent back results that were displayed on the terminal's screen.

UCSC soon upgraded to a Virtual Address eXtension (VAX) 11/780, a machine positioned by Digital Equipment Corporation as a successor to its PDP-11/70. It was roughly the size of a large safe and boasted 128 kilobytes of memory. The VAX was connected to rows of terminals within the cool, dimly lit computer labs around campus. Toy spent hours tinkering with the machine, pushing and prodding to learn its capabilities.

> Every time I came across a new computer, I tried to learn everything there was to it. In the modern era, you learn just enough to do what you need to do and then move on. You didn't do it that way back then. You learned everything.

His thirst for knowledge led him to a treasure trove of games supplied by the university's connection to ARPANET. One of the first games he pulled from the network was *Colossal Cave Adventure*, a text-only game. *Adventure* printed out descriptions of dark and mysterious caving systems and waited for players to type in what to do next. Even more than *Star Trek*, *Colossal Cave Adventure* made an indelible impression on Toy. He experienced a sense of wonder every time the VAX filled the terminal screen with descriptions of capacious rooms where stalagmites and stalactites laced together like the teeth of some great beast, of wind keening through caverns, of strange noises off in the distance.

"Computers. Computer games. The greatest things in the world," Toy stated simply.

> The things that were really exciting to me, though, as I became competent enough to program really interesting games, were the text adventures. For me, those moments [in text adventures] were actually more emotionally affecting than even modern computer

graphics. Maybe just now, the occasional game has an impact. Like the [underwater city] in *BioShock*—being there, in that world, changes you in a certain way.

Toy began writing his own text adventures. Nearby, he noticed another student doing the same thing.

"We met in the computer lab at UC Santa Cruz," Glenn Wichman recalled.[2]

> I was working on an adventure game that I was writing in BASIC. I was just teaching myself as I went along, and I made a big mess of it. Michael [Toy] looked over my shoulder and saw my game, and asked if he could play it. That begat a discussion.

Wichman was impressed by Toy's knowledge of computing. Toy had built his own desktop computer at home and had been writing games for several years. Wichman let Toy sift through his program while the two talked programming practices. "Most of what I know about programming, I know from working with him," Wichman reminisced during our interviews.

Although Toy had a leg up on Wichman in programming, Wichman was arguably more well-informed about how the moving parts of game design fit together. He had been creating board and card games to play with friends since the age of seven, and had revamped *Dungeons & Dragons* to accommodate a custom campaign based on C. S. Lewis's *The Chronicles of Narnia* novels. Repurposing the game had involved penning over 40 pages of customized rules that subverted *D&D*'s base guidelines, transforming it into a new experience.

When the time had come to select a college, Wichman had chosen UCSC deliberately. The school allowed students to create majors by cherry-picking from the course catalog. He had enrolled with the intention of inventing a major rooted in-game design that he could parlay into a career as a professional board-and-card-game creator. Discovering computers changed everything. "Once I discovered that you could play games on a computer, I quickly decided that was the better way to go, which is why I started to teach myself to program."

Toy and Wichman became fast friends. They split the cost of an apartment and spent as much time as possible writing and playing each other's games. Their favorites were text adventures. Wichman even wrote a program that let users assemble their own interactive stories by choosing from pre-assembled modules, all without writing a single line of code.

But Toy's interest in adventure games waned quickly. The problem was that the story and puzzles never changed; once he finished a game, there was no reason to boot it up a second time. Worse, he had no reason to play his own adventure games—he knew all the solutions. "The ideal would be to write a computer game that was fun for me to play, and that was the problem with these adventure games that I loved so much."

Irritated, Toy synced up to other University of California mainframes connected to the network and looked for other games to play. While deep-diving through files stored at UC Berkeley, 90 minutes away from the Santa Cruz campus, he found the answer to his game-programming prayers.

Curses and Cursors

In 1973, computer engineers Ken Thompson and Dennis Ritchie attended the Symposium on Operating System Principles at Purdue University. They were there to present a paper on

UNIX, the operating system they had created at AT&T's venerable Bell Labs facility. The tenet of UNIX was to provide users with a wide array of simple programs engineered to solve specific tasks. Ritchie had invented a new programming language called C, which he used to write UNIX as well as software that ran on the operating system. He made the language extensible, which enabled UNIX to run on a large variety of computer hardware.

Professor Bob Fabry traveled from UC Berkeley to hear the talk.[3] Impressed, he purchased a copy of UNIX for his school. He thought his students, especially those enrolled in his operating systems course, would enjoy experimenting with such a pliable OS. He was correct. Students who enrolled in a course grounded in studying and writing operating systems were all hardcore hackers, and Bill Joy was the most fervent among them. As soon as he got his hands on UNIX, Joy put together a small team of hackers and proceeded to modify nearly every facet of its code. In 1977, he distributed the Frankenstein OS around the campus, charging a nominal fee.[4] Anyone who obtained a copy was free to root around the code and submit improvements and custom software. Joy and his team filtered the cream of the crop and plugged them into future releases of the modified OS, which became known as Berkeley Software Distribution (BSD) UNIX.

By the time Toy and Wichman started at UC Santa Cruz, BSD UNIX had entered widespread usage across UC campuses and was branching out to other schools. Each new version of BSD, released on cassette tape, included handy programs written by Joy and other hackers. One program was curses, written by Ken Arnold. Arnold had written curses according to the UNIX creed: a simple tool fashioned for a specific purpose. Wielding curses like a paintbrush, users could place text such as letters, numbers, and symbols at any location on the screen.

The moment he used curses, Toy saw its potential. In 1980, he went to Wichman and suggested they use curses to create a graphical adventure game with a twist. Unlike *Colossal Cave Adventure* and its derivatives, their game would construct brand new environments and challenges every time. An avid *Dungeons & Dragons* player, he invented a fantasy-themed setting and premise. Players would assume the identity of an adventurer who entered the Dungeons of Doom, a series of levels filled with monsters and treasure.

Wichman loved the idea and dubbed the game *Rogue*.

> I think the name just came to me. Names needed to be short because you invoked a program by typing its name in a command line. I liked the idea of a rogue. We were coming from a *Dungeons & Dragons* background, but we were creating a single-player game. You weren't going down into the dungeon with a party. The idea was that this is a person going off on his or her own. It captured the theme very succinctly.

Apropos of UNIX, Toy chose to write *Rogue* in the C language. C produced fast code, while BASIC was slower and meant for smaller programs. Wichman, still a few steps behind Toy in programming prowess, learned C by watching Toy program their game. "The early alpha versions of *Rogue* were probably all my code, but Glenn [Wichman] made lots of contributions in terms of design," Toy recalled. "I think it's quite fair to say that the game was a pretty straight collaboration between Glenn [Wichman], Ken [Arnold], and me by the time it was done. I feel pretty good about that."

Where Are You @?

Toy and Wichman realized they wouldn't be able to stay at school during all hours to write their game. Fortunately, they didn't need to. As employees of the computer science division, they had special lab privileges. Setting up an ADM-3a terminal in their apartment, they could dial into the VAX 11/780 shunted off in a basement somewhere at UC Santa Cruz. The connection was established through their 300-baud modem—a device that would take several minutes to transmit the text on an average-length Wikipedia page today—enabling them to write the vast majority of *Rogue* from the comfort of their apartment.

Generating levels seemed the logical starting point for *Rogue*, so they thought about how best to display their dungeon hack. Coin-op hits such as *Pong*, *Space Invaders*, and *Asteroids* sported advanced graphics, but computers were still too slow and lacked the hardware to render swords and spaceships. Due to these restrictions, architecture in *Rogue* would be displayed from an overhead view, like looking down at a map, and the map would be drawn from text characters. Using Ken Arnold's curses library, they used periods (".") for floor tiles, dashes and vertical bars ("–" and "|") for walls, plus ("+") signs for doors, and hash marks ("#") for corridors that players could traverse.

The idea was to write code that functioned like a paintbrush, dipping into text characters and painting maps out of text symbols. Long corridors drawn from "#" signs would snake between rectangular rooms framed by "–" and "|" markings. The "+" doors would let users pass in and out of rooms and hallways, and onto "." floor tiles. Each finished map resembled a rudimentary blueprint.

To create levels that turned out differently every time they played, Toy and Wichman devised algorithms that assembled environments according to numbers chosen at random. Those numbers affected every square inch of dungeon real estate, from the size and number of rooms in each level to the curvature of the hallways that linked the rooms together. The effort was known among computer scientists as procedural generation, the practice of building content algorithmically rather than following plans that manufactured the same content every time.

Writing algorithms that generated clean levels was a process that took months to refine. Some early algorithms placed the staircase, which led down to the next dungeon, in rooms that were inaccessible to players. Other algorithms produced levels that were just plain ugly. "It's still sort of an unsolved problem: how to make interesting and complex spaces that are as engaging as something an artist designs, but able to spit out as many [pieces of content] as you need," Toy admitted.

> It's really hard to figure out, based on the computing resources you have, how to create worlds, and then design a world that is as amazing as something you could write or draw with your own hands. It's like trying to paint the Mona Lisa with an air cannon and a bucket of paint.

After hammering away at their algorithms, Toy and Wichman reached an elegant solution. "In *Rogue*, every level is a tic-tac-toe board; it's exactly nine rooms in a three-by-three grid,"

Wichman explained. "We basically divided the screen into those nine areas, and then put a room in each area." Level arrangements were incredibly diverse thanks to random numbers. Some rooms were long or wide; others were as poky as closets. Dungeons could have fewer than nine rooms, but never more than nine. Algorithms occasionally produced levels where rooms aligned neatly, but most dungeon configurations resembled a jigsaw puzzle with scrambled pieces.

As the algorithms for procedural generation took shape, Toy and Wichman entered their world and began to explore. The eponymous rogue was represented on the screen by an "@" sign, shorthand for "where you're at." Although the game was barely functional, Toy and Wichman had a blast moving their "@" avatars through empty, procedurally generated levels.

The next step was adding monsters to fight and treasures to collect.

Procedural Creativity

For *Rogue* to achieve Toy's dream of an infinitely replayable game, every element had to be procedurally generated. He and Wichman sprinkled weapons and magical items into the game's algorithms. Potions and scrolls tantalized. "We wanted to be able to be surprised by our own game. That's why, for example, when you find a scroll or portion, it's got a random flavor and name, and the correlation of the name to the flavor is hidden from the player," Wichman said. "That way, even we ourselves wouldn't know exactly what each potion would do. You could play one time and a lemon potion would [restore] health, and the next time, a cinnamon potion would [restore] health."

Not all effects were beneficial. Cursed items triggered negative effects such as leeching health or latching onto players permanently. For a long time, the only way to deduce an item's effects was to use it and wait anxiously to see what happened. Later on, Toy and Wichman added identification scrolls that spelled out the properties of unidentified items.

Populating the Dungeons of Doom with monsters was easy. Lifting monsters from *Dungeons & Dragons*, *Rogue*'s authors created kobolds, ogres, imps, bats, skeletons, leprechauns, and hordes of other enemies. Monsters were represented on the screen by capital letters, such as "B" for bat and "Z" for zombie. Aggressive enemies began to close the distance as soon as the player-character entered their line of sight, while others, such as monsters stationed by doors, waited for players to engage them. Players and monsters initiated combat by bumping into one another, but some foes inflicted harm through non-physical means. Leprechauns, for example, snatched gold, which impacted the player's final score. The variety of enemies threatened to overwhelm, but was made manageable through *Rogue*'s turn-based play, which gave players plenty of time to think encounters through.

Toy dreamed of creating monsters that came across as living, breathing entities able to adjust their behavior according to how players chose to confront them. While some monsters were infused with unique behavior, technology put down roadblocks. "I was using the biggest, fastest computer I could get my hands on, but it only had 128K of memory," he remembered. "I had a small set of items, dungeons drawn, and some monsters with a few different behaviors. The instructions base [of the computer] was full." Unable to ascribe more interesting characteristics to the majority of monsters, Toy and Wichman simply gave more health and stronger attacks to monsters higher up on the food chain.

Once *Rogue* became playable, they invited regulars in the computer labs to try their hands at the game. To their astonishment, the imaginations of their players filled in the blanks left by inadequate technology. "People would invent meaning," Toy remembered.

> They would place themselves in this situation and their creativity would express itself. They made the world more interesting and beautiful. So even though the thing I created wasn't beautiful, people would color it with their own imagination, in the same way you do when playing a text adventure. I'd listen to someone explain how to play the game to someone else, and they'd start talking about something that was completely ridiculous and made up. They'd say, 'Here's how this particular monster thinks.' And I'm thinking, *That monster? He's one of the non-thinking monsters.*

Wichman likewise observed players inventing strategies for survival. Bats, for example, moved in a zigzag pattern meant to imitate their wild fluttering. Crafty players realized they could defeat bats easily by luring them into tight corridors. With no room to weave around, bats were helpless to dodge arrows. "We didn't design the game or bat with that strategy in mind. It's just that bats flutter as bats do. People playing it came up with that strategy for beating them."

Ferocious capital letters moving around on the screen sparked the interest of players who dwelled in the UCSC computer labs, and *Rogue*'s high mortality rate poured kerosene on the flames. When players died in *Rogue*, their character was irretrievably lost. The concept became known as permadeath. "All video games, in the mind of my grumpy, curmudgeonly self, were: to win this game, just go up, up, left, right," Toy said.

> [Games were] just a series of moves with timing in between them. Execute them in the right order and you win. Permadeath was an attempt to make that go away. You're in *this* instant, and you can't make a mistake and try again. If you're going to make a character that wins, you have to be somebody who knows when to run away, or your character is dead.

Early versions of *Rogue* had to be finished in one sitting. Later, Toy and Wichman added the option for players to save their progress. After discovering that some players were save scumming, the process of making copies of their saved data so they could keep playing if their character died, Toy and Wichman changed the code so that it erased characters immediately upon death. "I do remember that, because of each interaction with monsters, if the last move you made was, 'I swing at the monster and miss; he swings and hits,' you could just [restore progress] and keep playing that sequence until the odds were in your favor," Wichman said. "We wanted to make it realistic."

With each new element Toy and Wichman wrote into *Rogue*, the game became more and more absorbing. Rather than reveal the entire dungeon map when players set foot in a new level, the game showed only their immediate surroundings. Moving in any direction revealed more of the map—and the creatures lying in wait. The graphics were primitive, but the thrill and apprehension of exploring uncharted terrain, combined with the pseudo-intelligent behavior of the monsters and the permanency of death, drew players deeper into the fantasy.

"We [printed] descriptions as things happened to you, and we had various monsters that we created, and potions, and things like that," Wichman remembered.

> It was interesting that we did end up having an atmosphere even though all you're looking at is letters and symbols. We got drawn into the world, and you would imagine yourself in

the world. You'd see a letter 'T' on the screen, and it would startle you because you knew it was a troll.

Adventurers braved the Dungeons of Doom on the loose premise of recovering a MacGuffin called the Amulet of Yendor. Toy viewed the premise as trivial. His hope was that players would find greater enjoyment in recounting their own adventures.

> The main thing I was trying to create was moments of panic and terror, and every moment [feeling] really important. Like, 'This moment right now is really important, and I need to survive it to get to the next moment.' That story would be something you could only tell in retrospect. You can construct a broader story afterwards, kind of like you don't know the broader story of your life until you've had time to look back and say, 'Oh, so that's what happened.' The Amulet was completely unimportant in any way, shape, or form. There just needed to be a reason to send you down there.

Best of all, *Rogue* was having the same effect on Toy and Wichman as it was having on their growing legion of testers. They, like everyone else, fell in love with figuring out how to hit *Rogue*'s curveballs. "There was no real design. We just said, 'Let's make the monsters progressively harder and see how it goes.'" Toy said.

> Once you figured out the mechanics of the game, you could usually get down to the midteens [dungeon levels]. Anybody could do that. Just don't be stupid. If you're in trouble, run away, heal up, come back and fight things.

Wichman agreed.

> We especially liked when the game would surprise us. I can't remember a specific [anecdote], just general recollections of, 'Hey, did you realize that if you do this, this other thing will end up happening?' That wasn't something we necessarily designed. It was just some consequence of how the world we'd created ended up working that we hadn't anticipated.

Forked

Toy and Wichman failed to notice their transcendence from lowly students to local celebrities when *Rogue* began circulating around UC Santa Cruz. The game was still a work in progress. They continued writing code, brainstorming ideas, and collecting feedback from fellow students who were spending more and more of their time playing the game. According to Wichman,

> Getting the feedback was fun. We were admired a lot for being the ones who were coming up with this. It was an ego boost, and it was also just a lot of fun to get feedback, to watch people play the game, and to make adjustments and see whether they were accepted or rejected.

Realizing that the mere act of surviving in *Rogue* would become a badge of pride and status around campus, Toy and Wichman implemented a scoreboard in one of the earliest iterations of the game. The board recorded the top ten scores, ranking players according to how much gold they had collected and how far they had descended at the moment of their death. "Remember all that stuff I said about getting the Amulet not meaning anything?" Toy asked me.

> Forget everything I said. I wanted winning the game to be an achievement. If you got the Amulet, that would be something worth telling your friends about, unlike most computer games, which you just play until you've put enough hours into them and then you're done.

Shortly after *Rogue* started making the rounds, Toy's focus on computers and games caught up with him. His grades got him kicked out of UC Santa Cruz. He lined up a job in the computer labs at UC Berkeley, where he hoped that pursuing knowledge of computers in return for a paycheck instead of grades would serve him better.

Just like that, Wichman's best friend was gone. Furthermore, Toy's departure planted a fork in the road of *Rogue*'s development. "Things weren't set up to share source code so we could work collaboratively. I had my version of *Rogue* at Santa Cruz, and Michael had his version at Berkeley," said Wichman. "Occasionally, we would send ideas to each other."

Wichman did his best to keep up with his version of *Rogue*. He added the concept of armor, represented as a "]" bracket, and fiddled with a few other features. Eventually, he was forced to call it quits.

> Michael transferred to Berkeley and took Rogue with him. That's when Ken Arnold got involved. After a while, I stopped working on it. It became Michael's and Ken's project until a few years later when we decided to make a commercial version of it.

*   *   *

Side Quests

(Turn to page 23 for Chapter 3)

Make Your Own Adventure

Wichman's goal in creating a design program for adventure games was to let anyone write interactive fiction regardless of their familiarity with computers.

> Basically, each room would be in its own file. You could enter a room description [for a room] and list key objects in the room along with exits. You could say 'This exit is blocked' or 'You must have a certain item in your inventory to use this exit,' some conditional statements like those.

Wichman viewed *Rogue* as more of a tactical gaming experience, like chess. Writing adventure games, and his do-it-yourself adventure kit, was an outlet for his creativity. He wrote early versions in the BASIC language then switched to Pascal.

New School

Contemporary takes on *Rogue*, such as *Classic Rogue* by Oryx Design Lab, replace the original game's text characters with tiles and sprites. Later versions of *Rogue* written by Toy, Wichman, and their friend Jon Lane would also feature graphics.

"I would have made it graphical from the beginning if the technology had been available to us," Wichman said, who admitted that he understands why some users prefer the text-only esthetic.

> I think there is a nostalgic feeling to character graphics, and that was something I put back into the Atari ST version. In the Mac version, you could only play in graphics mode. When I did the Atari ST version, I put a classic mode in the preferences menu so you could go back to how it looked on the original UNIX machines. The ST came with a fairly small monitor, so as an excuse, it was like, 'Okay, you want to see more of the map on the screen at once, you can put the game in classic mode to view the whole map.'

(Author's Note: Users interested in trying *Classic Rogue* can find it at http://oryxdesignlab.com/rogue/.)

"@" Through the @ges

Known for its starring role in email addresses, Twitter handles, and bravely venturing into procedurally generated dungeons, the "@" sign has a mysterious past.[5] According to a short history published by *Smithsonian* magazine, the first recorded instance of the symbol occurred in 1536 when a Florentine merchant by the name of Francesco Lapi used "@" to represent units of amphorae, a wine. The symbol became more prolific in commerce to denote "at the rate of," such as "4 pieces @ $2."

Smithsonian traced the symbol's usage in technology back to 1971. That year, Ray Tomlinson, a computer scientist employed by BBN Technologies, was trying to figure out how to address messages between senders and receivers connected to ARPANET. His challenge was to designate a symbol on the keyboard not already widely used by computers. Studying the keyboard, Tomlinson happened to notice the @ sign, saving the little-used key from certain extinction.

An "@" Named Rodney

Players enter *Rogue*'s Dungeons of Doom on the premise of recovering an artifact called the Amulet of Yendor. Yendor is Rodney spelled backwards, an anagram Toy dashed off without giving it much thought. According to Wichman, Rodney played a bigger role.

> Initially, Rodney was the name of the adventurer that you were playing. I think that got lost somewhere along the line, and probably for good reason, because people want to play as themselves, not Rodney. I never gave any thought as to the relationship of Rodney to Yendor. Maybe he was some long-lost, black-sheep relative. Those would be fun details if they made *Rogue* into a movie or something.

Stages of Grief

In many ways, *Rogue*'s gameplay mechanics were as simple as its veneer of text characters. Players did not choose races and classes such as human, paladin, orc, or ranger. They simply named their adventurer and increased basic stats such as strength as they advanced through the dungeons. That simplicity kept Wichman from mourning for too long when his characters inevitably met their match.

> I didn't imbue my characters with personality or unique names or anything like that. There were certainly times when I'd gotten down to the 24th or 25th level, or I'd retrieved the Amulet and was on my way back up, and I got killed. I was very upset because I got so close. *Rogue* is more akin to chess. You don't name your pieces. It's a little more abstract than some of its successors, especially compared to the graphical games you have now.

Save Scumming

Given *Rogue*'s harsh penalty for failure, Toy and Wichman knew they would have to stay two steps ahead of players attempting to create backup versions of their characters, a process known as save scumming. "*Rogue* [ran] on a time-sharing system," Toy explained, referencing how users partitioned storage on systems that ran UNIX. "You had your own set of files, but there were all sorts of restrictions on what you could do to the system. We just took advantage of that."

Toy and Wichman did their best to circumvent save scumming by structuring files in ways known only to them. "The main thing we did was that every file had a unique identifier," Toy said.

> When we looked at a save file, we added a few [memory-related] characters and could see when it was written, so when we opened it up, we could check to see if it was still the same save file when we wrote it. If it had changed in any way, it wasn't the original file. You couldn't copy it, rename it, or open it. The only place where you could manipulate it was your computer where you had administrator privileges. So nobody who didn't own their own system managed to defeat the copy protection.

Notes

1. I grew up in Livermore, California: Interview with Michael Toy. All quotes from Michael Toy come from interviews conducted via phone, Skype, and email over 2012–2014.
2. We met in the computer lab at UC Santa Cruz: Interview with Glenn Wichman. All quotes from Glenn Wichman come from interviews conducted via Skype and email over 2012–2014.
3. Professor Bob Fabry traveled from UC Berkeley: "Twenty Years of Berkeley UNIX." *O'Reilly*. http://oreilly.com/catalog/opensources/book/kirkmck.html.
4. In 1977, he distributed the Frankenstein OS: "Berkeley Engineers: Changing Our World." *Berkeley Engineering: Lab Notes*. http://coe.berkeley.edu/labnotes/history_unix.html.
5. Most known for its starring role in email addresses: "The Accidental History of the @ Symbol." *Smithsonian*. http://www.smithsonianmag.com/science-nature/the-accidental-history-of-the-symbol-18054936/?no-ist. (Author's note: This reference can be found in the Side Quest supplementary material for this chapter.)

3

Rodney and the Free Market
Building Rogue, *Part 2*

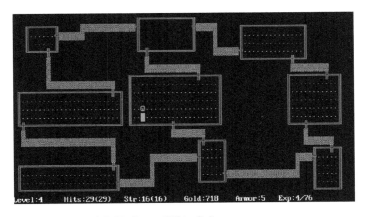

Rogue: The Adventure Game running on MS-DOS. (Image: Wikipedia.)

Arbiters

Ken C. R. C. Arnold grew up in a household where science and technology were as common-place as dishware. During the early 1970s, his father worked as a programmer and scientist in charge of writing computer simulations. Arnold took an interest in his father's work and peppered him with questions. One day, Arnold's father stanched his son's tide of inquiries by handing him a book on FORTRAN, a programming language designed to solve scientific computations quickly and efficiently.

Excited to dig in, Arnold studied the first lesson. The objective was to write a program that generated a Fibonacci sequence, a string of numbers where each successive number is the sum of the previous two numbers: {0, 1, 1, 2, 3, 5, 8, 13}. Generating a Fibonacci sequence had long been considered an arduous trial for burgeoning programmers, one meant to test their grasp of logic more than their command over language syntax. Most programmers needed three vari-ables—containers for data such as numbers and text—to generate a Fibonacci sequence: two variables to hold one term apiece, and a third to hold their sum. The program then entered a loop, calculating sums and constructing a long sequence of Fibonacci terms by passing terms and sums between the three variables until it reached a designated stopping point or the user terminated the program.

To his father's amazement, Arnold solved the problem in record time—using only two variables. "I thought memory was precious," Arnold explained in our interview.

> So I told my dad, and he said, 'You can't do that with two variables.' I said, 'Yes, you can. Look.' He looked at it and said, 'You're right.' And I thought, *My god. I might be better at this than he is.* For any teenager, that is a great temptation.

Arnold's quick learning pushed him to seek out new challenges in computing. He spent most of his time at school sharpening his programming skills and playing the same *Star Trek* game that had captured Michael Toy's imagination. When he and other students exhausted the school's supply of games, they wrote their own. Still in high school, he learned that his community's chapter of Eagle Scouts routinely met at a company that allowed access to their computers. Arnold suddenly became very interested in earning merit badges.

Following graduation, Arnold decided to take a year off between high school and college. He got a job at Lawrence Berkeley National Laboratory located near UC Berkeley's campus. When he was not working alongside his colleague, Art Rosenfeld, who designed programs that calculated how much energy a building would consume in a diverse range of climates, he trawled UC Berkeley's computer lab. Arnold was eager to jump on the lab's PDP-11/70 minicomputers, and tutored students in exchange for an account at the lab. Up to 40 students could connect to a single 11/70 via a modem, and were allotted 50 kilobytes of disk space, enough capacity for Arnold to write some interesting programs in C.

While 50K of disk space was considered plentiful for the late 1970s, UC Berkeley's computers came up short in other ways. Every user connected to the PDP-11/70 worked at a dumb terminal, and each screen displayed information in the same way: as new text appeared on the screen, old text got pushed up and out of view. Once it was gone, it was gone for good. The cursor operated similarly: it sat at the position where the next keyboard character would appear, unable to be maneuvered around the screen so users could correct typos or expand on previous paragraphs.

The arrival of cursor-addressable terminals at UC Berkeley was a game changer. Unlike ordinary dumb terminals, cursor-addressable terminals divided the screen into a grid of rows and columns, and tracked where each character on the grid was stored in memory. In other words, savvy programmers could move the cursor to any square in the grid and modify or add text there.

Such a radical leap forward in display technology gave rise to all sorts of programming possibilities. In 1976, Bill Joy, the hacker who would lead development of BSD UNIX, wrote a text editor called vi, short for "visual," that allowed users to move their cursor and edit text anywhere on the screen.

Other, non-academic programs took advantage of cursor-addressable terminals. In 1963, the American Standards Association created the American Standard Code for Information Interchange, or ASCII. ASCII is a collection of text characters such as letters, numbers, and symbols commonly found on keyboards. Arnold and other students realized they could use ASCII characters to create graphics.

My friends and I would write these little programs that would use the cursor library to do something visually interesting. A guy drew a little ASCII picture of a car, and you could watch it drive across the screen. I ended up writing a little impersonation of a fly that buzzed around the screen.

Animating flies and automobiles consisted of grouping individual ASCII characters together so they resembled images, then erasing the screen and re-plotting the characters to new locations over and over, simulating movement.

Cursor-addressable terminals came with one downside. Each terminal stored characters differently, so programmers had to rewrite cursor-addressable code on every type of cursor-addressable terminal they used. Tired of revising code every time a new terminal appeared in the lab, Arnold wrote a platform-agnostic library of cursor functions. He called his library curses.

Keepers of the Code

When Bill Joy corralled worthy programs and packaged them in BSD UNIX in 1978, curses received a place of honor. By 1980, *Rogue* had spread from its home on UC Santa Cruz's computers to other UC campuses, including UC Berkeley. Arnold took to the game right away.

> People often believe that curses was written for *Rogue* because most people saw them at the same time. We were playing *Rogue*, and somebody came up to me at one point and said, 'You know, *Rogue* is really, really smart. When you move on the screen, it only redraws the characters it has to redraw.' I said, 'Oh, they must be using curses.'

Arnold enjoyed *Rogue* but grew frustrated with its interface. For as smart as other users believed the game was, it used resource-heavy methods of cleaning up the screen. The modems that connected dumb terminals to the lab's minicomputers were 300 bauds, which meant the minicomputers could only send 30 characters to the screen per second. *Rogue*'s usage of curses to reposition the cursor and redraw the dungeon every time the screen refreshed was painfully slow.

As much as Arnold wanted to tighten up the game, his hands were tied. *Rogue*'s creators, two students from UCSC named Michael Toy and Glenn Wichman, had opted not to make their code freely available. Then, in 1982, a new employee joined UC Berkeley's lab and started asking around after Arnold. "Mike Toy transferred to Berkeley, which I didn't know about until he came and looked me up," Arnold explained. Toy, he found out, was aware that Arnold had written curses, and had sought him out to learn more about how the library worked. "We started exchanging ideas. Over time, we got to know each other well enough that he trusted me with the code," Arnold said.

For Arnold, the first order of business was popping *Rogue*'s hood and optimizing the code.

> What it used to do every time you [opened the] inventory was clear the screen, draw the inventory, then clear the screen [when you closed the inventory] and redraw the map. One of the first things I did was display the inventory in the upper-right corner of the screen as far to the right as I could. That meant that the least amount of screen area had to be erased.

I would clear out that area, draw the inventory, and when you were done, I'd only have to redraw that area [of the map].

Arnold and Toy put their heads together and made dozens of other improvements. Long, winding corridors connected *Rogue*'s tic-tac-toe arrangement of rooms, but were tedious to navigate. Players had to hold down a movement key in one direction, wait until they hit a wall, then move in another direction, and so on until they finally came to a room. Arnold rewrote the code so the "@" avatar raced through hallways automatically, halting only if it encountered an object that required the player's attention, such as a monster or a treasure in the passage. Arnold modified the interface further, cutting down on verbs used to describe battles. When he finished, the game output "You hit" or "Monster hit," where monster was a specific creature such as a kobold or zombie. Although the output was less interesting, Arnold reasoned that players wanted to spend less time reading text outputs to find relevant data and more time exploring the Dungeons of Doom.

Level generation, while inexpensive in terms of hardware resources, received an overhaul. "When you went up [the stairs], you appeared in a different level. You didn't return to the same place," Arnold explained. Adding a dose of realism, he modified the code so that going back up staircases returned players to dungeons they had cleared. Other new content proved more substantial. The code Toy had carried to UC Berkeley included 30 possible names for scrolls. Arnold added syllables that the game selected randomly for even greater variety. The two friends also added rings and amulets that could be worn to add beneficial effects—provided they weren't cursed—as well as magical staffs for players who preferred spells over steel.

As the game's content base grew richer, Arnold and Toy knew that prestige for conquering the dungeons would swell in turn. "There was a score file, so we tried really hard to make it that if you didn't at least have root [administrative] privileges, you couldn't cheat the score file," Arnold explained. "I didn't mind if you cheated, but you can't record that score and have other people play against it. That was my attitude about it."

Widespread Distribution

When Bill Joy and the other members of the BSD UNIX committee gathered programs for the release of version 4.2 of their operating system, they rounded out the package by asking others what programs they would like to see included. Besides the usual assortment of productivity tools, BSD UNIX shipped with a games folder that contained the likes of chess and a few quizzes. *Rogue* made the cut, and was distributed as part of 4.2BSD in 1984.[1]

As the number of computers tethered to ARPANET and other networks grew, BSD UNIX became ubiquitous, finding a home in computer labs all over the world. Arnold and Toy occasionally received letters from professionals and students who were enjoying *Rogue*'s addictive and danger-laden levels. Every so often, fans contacted them from the most unlikely of places. "There was somebody who worked at a nuclear bomb laboratory in Nevada, and you think, *Shouldn't they be doing something besides playing games when nuclear weapons are at stake?*" Arnold remembered. "To a certain extent, it also felt like, if *Rogue* was interfering with weapon development, maybe that's a good thing. Maybe it's good that we were slowing all that down."

As pleasantly bewildering as it was to hear from technicians at nuclear labs, Toy and Arnold were utterly bowled over when they learned that their computing heroes enjoyed *Rogue*. Ken Thompson, a computer scientist at Bell Labs who co-created UNIX alongside Dennis Ritchie, apparently played the game so much that he had taken time out of his schedule to hack the encryption scheme Arnold had written. "When it really hit me was, somebody who worked in Bell Labs said, 'Ken Thompson does the following thing to cheat,'" Arnold remembered. "I was like, 'Oh. I had no idea Ken Thompson enjoyed the game. This is a really big thing.'"

In 1984, Arnold graduated from UC Berkeley and took a job at UC San Francisco as a developer. He and Toy, who had already landed a job at Italian typewriter manufacturer Olivetti, took *Rogue*'s source code with them. They envisioned turning the game into a commercial product. Looking back, Arnold regrets their attitude. "Unfortunately, since we took the source with us, other people weren't able to take it and do something with it."

Time passed, and Arnold and Toy lost track of *Rogue*'s code. The dream of converting *Rogue* into a commercial product was lost.

Typewriters and Mainframes

Olivetti was founded as a typewriter manufacturer in 1908 by Camillo Olivetti, an electrical engineer residing in Italy. By 1930, Olivetti's son Adriano had taken charge, and eyed a new business. The company produced and sold an electric calculator, the Divisumma, in 1948, and built Italy's first mainframe computer, the Elea 9003, in 1959. In 1965, Olivetti broke new ground when it released the Programma 101, the world's first desktop computer, which looked like a typewriter-sized adding machine.[2]

Even though the Programma 101 was small enough to sit on a desk, mainframes still ran Olivetti's offices and laboratories, and BSD UNIX was the company's operating system of choice. One of the chief administrators at Olivetti's United States location was Jon Lane. "This was my second job after college and during the UNIX days," Lane told me. "UNIX was just getting out into the real world, and of course, people from universities had more experience [using UNIX] than people in the industry, so I was able to do whatever I wanted if it involved UNIX."

Just like on UC campuses, BSD UNIX ran on mainframes and supported dozens of users who dialed in through dumb terminals. BSD UNIX supported multiple users by way of time-sharing, the process of carving up a mainframe's cycles of operation among all the users dialed in to it. More users logged on meant fewer cycles for each user, which meant more waiting between actions. Part of Lane's job entailed monitoring cycles to see which programs ate up the most time. A few months into his tenure, a new program appeared in his reports. "There was a group of people running Olivetti's network, and *Rogue* came up as the number-one used [program] on the network. More CPU cycles went to *Rogue* than anything else."

Lane saw no harm in *Rogue* since the game ate up a very small percentage of cycles during Olivetti's hours of operation. After work, most of the engineers would stay over to play. Lane joined in happily, caught up in *Rogue*'s risk-reward design. When business took him to Olivetti headquarters in Italy, he had a fortuitous encounter. "I went to Italy to install some stuff, and Michael [Toy] was also working for Olivetti as a consultant. Michael and I became fast friends.

I said, 'Hey, your game is unbelievable. We should get that running on the PC that just came out.'"

Toy saw potential in Lane's pitch. More powerful than competing hardware such as the Apple II, the PC was becoming the platform of choice for businesses looking to adopt word processors and spreadsheets. Game developers found merit in the PC as well. Toy and Lane founded a company called Artificial Intelligence Design. Toy had salvaged *Rogue*'s source code from UC Berkeley, but it amounted to a sketch on a cocktail napkin instead of a fully realized blueprint. "Michael [Toy] had the source code, but I definitely had to rewrite [a lot of the game]," Lane recalled. "We didn't have curses, so I had to rewrite all the [text output] libraries."

Functionally, the PC version of *Rogue*—titled *Rogue: The Adventure Game*—behaved like the original version. Esthetically, it exhibited several changes. DOS, the dominant operating system on the PC, supported a set of characters called Code page 437, or CP437 for short. On top of the familiar array of letters, numbers, and symbols, CP437 featured special characters such as the diamond, heart, spade, and club playing-card iconography.

Thanks to CP437's plethora of special characters, the PC version of *Rogue* was a visually impressive game, though still primitive. Uppercase letters once again stood for trolls and other monsters, but symbols replaced other previously text-based representations. Instead of an "@," players controlled a smiley face. Dungeon walls were made up of solid brown bars, and meandering stretches of white-and-black squares stood for corridors that connected rooms. A yellow asterisk symbolized gold coins. The Amulet of Yendor, the object of every *Rogue* player's desire, appeared as a golden ankh.

Since Toy and Lane intended to sell *Rogue*, they made several changes to stay out from under the watchful eyes of the lawyers who represented *Dungeons & Dragons* publisher TSR. Kobolds and Xorns, two of the many monsters that *Rogue* lifted straight from the pages of the *Dungeons & Dragons Monster Manual*, were replaced by generic yet powerful monsters like the kestrel, a falcon-like bird of prey.

Friendly Rivalry

When the game was finished, Lane and Toy paid out of their own pockets to advertise to PC owners. *Rogue* sold more copies each time they stepped up advertising, but they still barely broke even. They lacked the deep pockets necessary to secure shelf space dominated by big distributors such as Merisel. To their surprise, developers at Epyx wanted to help *Rogue* carve out a spot on store shelves. Based in San Francisco, Epyx published action and role-playing games for a wide range of desktop computers. A few of the developers had tried *Rogue* for PC, loved it, and urged Robert Botch, vice president of marketing, to license the game for other platforms.

Botch took a look at the game and raised an eyebrow. "*Rogue* was a concern to many people on my staff due to its apparent niche appeal and lack of graphics," he explained to me. Still, Botch decided to trust the taste of Epyx's engineers and contracted A.I. Design to bring *Rogue* to the Apple Macintosh and Commodore Amiga.

If we focused on more core gamers and limited our costs, we thought it might be profitable. And I would imagine, as usually happened in the business, we had a title or two that was behind schedule [leaving room in the lineup for *Rogue*].

Toy and Lane divvied up the work. Since Lane had done most of the heavy lifting on the PC version, Toy, who was eager to put his new Macintosh through its paces, handled development of the Apple version. The Mac had several advantages over the PC. Apple's operating system featured a graphical user interface (GUI) where users got around by clicking on icons, whereas DOS required users to type in commands. The Mac also sported more memory and a faster processor. A.I. Design could distinguish the Mac version of *Rogue* by including graphics that resembled characters and monsters. This raised a new issue: neither Toy nor Lane had art skills decent enough to be featured in a commercial product.

To give the Mac version the treatment it deserved, Toy reached out to an old friend. "The PC version still used character graphics, but for the Mac version, I drew all the characters," Glenn Wichman said. "That was me. That was my contribution: I did all the graphics for that version. They were black-and-white, 25-by-25 pixels."

Despite his interest in working on the game again, Wichman returned to the *Rogue* fold warily. After dropping development of the original incarnation of the game at UC Santa Cruz, he had missed out on the exposure *Rogue* had given Toy, Arnold, and Lane. It was a sore spot for Wichman that he had been given a perfunctory mention in the credits of the PC version, which read *The game of Rogue was originated by Michael C. Toy and Kenneth C.R.C. Arnold—Adapted for the IBM PC by Jon Lane—Significant Contributions by Glenn Wichman and scores of others*. In effect, he'd been lumped in with nameless college kids who had suggested changes to the game during its development at UC campuses.

When a snowstorm buried Lake Tahoe under a blanket of cold, Toy and Wichman got a chance to bond. Lane and Toy had season passes at Squaw Valley. Renting a cabin, they hit the slopes while Wichman, who had no interest in skiing, remained behind in the warmth of the cabin and drew walls, doors, monsters, weapons, and quivers of arrows. At night, they wrote code for the Mac and discussed design ideas with Wichman, whose trepidation at reuniting with Toy thawed in the face of the excitement and challenge of engineering a new version of *Rogue*.

"The next big change came with the Macintosh version, where we embraced the Mac idea of a windowed GUI, with separate windows for inventory, map, status, and overhead view, also mouse-based point-and-click movement," Wichman explained. A greater use of graphical elements made *Rogue* appear more modern. The player's remaining life was displayed as a graphical bar that drained as the player-character—now represented by a small knight—took damage.

Snow began to fall over Squaw Valley, first at a serene trickle and then in a torrent. Inside, the A.I. Design trio fell into a cozy pattern of exploring the snow-covered mountains by day and working through the night. When they ran up against technical barriers like the Mac's paltry amount of memory, they leafed through stacks of computing magazines in search of optimization techniques. "It was a funny time when software engineers were doing things on their own," Lane reminisced. "The software industry hadn't gelled yet, the way it did when

Microsoft started taking out all the private citizens like us who were trying to make some kind of dent in the software world."

The contract between A.I. Design and Epyx afforded Toy and Lane a modest sum for each version of *Rogue* they produced. As payment for the artwork used in the Macintosh version, Wichman was given the Mac he had used to create artwork, a payment he felt was commensurate to his contributions.[3] Around the same time, Epyx offered to let Wichman helm the adaptation of the game to the Atari ST. Wichman accepted the offer and got to work on an Atari ST provided by Epyx. The computer sported a dual floppy-disk drive; no hard drive was available. One disk drive held the C compiler on which Wichman wrote code, and the other held the game that took shape over several weeks.

Since neither Toy nor Lane were interested in working on an Atari ST, Wichman had carte blanche over his adaptation of *Rogue*. He turned all artistic contributions over to Michael Kosaka, an in-house artist at Epyx whom Wichman felt was better suited to harness the ST's deeper color palette, and focused on design. *Rogue*'s core gameplay remained the same, although Wichman did add in new secrets for players to discover such as the centaur's ability to curse the player's armor and items.

For Wichman, the opportunity to leave an indelible mark on *Rogue* was the final board he needed to mend old fences.

> Michael [Toy] was doing the Amiga version. We worked side by side and had a friendly rivalry going to see who could come up with the better version. That started to remind people that a lot of *Rogue*'s ideas were mine, and that I was a bigger part of [the game] than I got credit for. Once the Atari ST version was out, I could say, 'I did this version. *Rogue* is just as much mine as it is anybody's.' I no longer felt bad about being left out.

Legacy

Robert Botch and his marketing team took a different tack when the time came to market the handful of *Rogue* ports published by Epyx.

> We felt the game would not sell well through our main distribution channels which were Toys R Us, K-B Toys, Kmart, Target, and other mass merchants. Action games with high graphic content were the type of titles these retailers wanted to sell because that is what their customers were buying.

Knowing that the average consumer judged a game by flipping the box over to check out the screenshots on the back, Botch played it safe and distributed *Rogue* through software catalogs.

Rogue enjoyed a transitory stay in the upper ranks of Merisel's catalog, then dropped off and faded away. Everyone put forth their reasoning for why the game failed to catch on in the mass market. Robert Botch said he found the game tricky to market. Magazine advertisements were out of the question. Those demographics consisted of casual gamers who put stock in flashy graphics and shied away from gameplay mechanics like permadeath.

Wichman's gut reaction was to blame software pirates, but years of reflection caused him to come to terms with tough truths. Unlike many games of the era, *Rogue* had no sound, no animations, and no distinct character classes such as paladins and archers, which gave players access to unique play styles and strategies. In *Rogue*, every player-character was more or less the same. Plus, he, Toy, and Arnold had set a precedent years ago while at university.

> The people who made it the most popular game on campuses in the early '80s were used to playing it for free. The idea was we would give them that same experience on their home computer, but charge them money for it. I think that wasn't the audience that was looking for games in software stores.

For Ken Arnold, *Rogue* worked better as a conversation starter that afforded him the opportunity to have interesting conversations.

> Michael [Toy] and I gave a talk in Boston on *Rogue*, and on the value of games in a work environment. It was a packed talk. Everybody was there to see it, and I really enjoyed it. You enjoy people liking what you did, and hearing, 'Oh, your idea gave me the idea to do this.' I really enjoy that.

Wichman waved off *Rogue*'s commercial failure and the modest payments he received. To him, the game means something more.

> The total income I made from *Rogue* is $15,000—advances on royalties for the Atari ST version. But *Rogue* also gave me a career; *Rogue* was my diploma, *Rogue* was my resume. And somehow *Rogue* just kept hanging in there, year after year; people kept playing it, kept porting it, kept adding on and improving it. We didn't set out to invent a genre, but that's what ended up happening, and I feel so blessed to have been a seminal part of that.

Jon Lane simply appreciates that he was able to go along for the ride.

> *PC World* put *Rogue* for the PC as the sixth best game of all time.[4] I get to say that's *my* version, but not really. Michael [Toy], Glenn [Wichman], and Ken [Arnold] were the geniuses behind the game, and Michael put together the idea that random numbers would make the game different every time. That one little thing made *Rogue* one of the most important games ever. Every once in a while, and even now, I hear people talking about *Rogue* and how great it was. I never jump into those conversations, but I do hear them, and I kind of laugh.

The Michael Toy

Michael Toy, curmudgeonly by his own admission, feels twangs of regret when he looks back on *Rogue*. He marveled at the imagination and beauty that players injected into the game, but lamented that most monsters were simple automatons differentiated only by how hard they hit. "*Moria* is probably the closest to what I wanted to do when I made *Rogue*. It's got shops, and all the monsters are really different. When I played *Moria*, I felt more like, yeah, this is what I wanted to get *Rogue* to do."

Ironically, *Rogue*'s failure to attract notice from mainstream gamers did not keep the game from leaving an impression on gaming culture and mainstream technology. So complex was

Rogue, with so many moving parts, that a professor at UC Santa Cruz used the source code as an illustration of how complex programs work.

Even so, it was a chance meeting at USENIX, an annual conference where technology professionals gather to discuss trends in computing, that allowed *Rogue* to take on greater personal significance for Toy, as well as attain a profound level of historical significance for the computing industry. Toy, attending with Lane, hobnobbed with pioneers such as Bill Joy, Ken Thompson—and Toy's idol, Dennis Ritchie, co-creator of UNIX and the author of the C programming language. Lane recounted the story of Ritchie's and Toy's meeting. "Dennis Ritchie was talking to us, and someone said, 'Dennis, this is Michael Toy,'. And Dennis Ritchie is the god of UNIX, right? So Dennis looks at Michael and says, '*The* Michael Toy?' Michael looked at him and said, 'I can die and go to heaven.'"

As the conversation went on, Ritchie jocularly accused *Rogue* of being responsible for the single greatest waste of CPU cycles in history.[5] Toy was thrilled.

> Dennis Ritchie, one of the administrators, had his own system. We talked to him about *Rogue* once, and he said he figured out how to get around the copy-protection system. One of the early alphas of *Rogue* that was posted up on UC Santa Cruz was discovered, and I still don't know exactly how. Someone hacked our labs. They renamed the binary from '*Rogue*' to '*UBL*' for *Under Bell Labs*. It had quite a big following at Bell Labs as *UBL*, and I didn't even know about it. All of those people were my heroes. They made UNIX, and they were playing *Rogue*.

*   *   *

Side Quests

(Turn to page 37 for Chapter 4)

Like Father, Like Son

Having dabbled in software development during our time in high school and university, my editor and I expressed curiosity at how Ken Arnold had managed to generate the Fibonacci sequence—a stumbling block for many green programmers—so efficiently.

"Oh, it's just a trick," Arnold explained. "There are three values, but they are related, so you can always recreate one from the other two. My father just assumed I had misunderstood something. I wrote the program on paper at home so I couldn't test it. Remember, FORTRAN was on punched cards for room-sized computers (1973). So if I was wrong on my very first program, who would be surprised? I think he said something like 'You can't do that.' But when he read it and figured it out, he was amused, and I suspect a little proud, or maybe the right word is the Yiddish naches: pleasure in the accomplishments of your children. He was never one to be upset to be proved wrong; he took it as learning something new. He did say that it was harder to read, and memory wasn't expensive at the level of a local variable or two. Which, now that I think of it, was my first lesson in the value of programming style."

"Thanks in any case for a reason to think about my father, which is always a pleasure for me."

Tactics

Thanks to *Rogue*'s randomized nature, not even Toy and Arnold's intimate knowledge of the game's inner workings proved much help. In fact, Arnold viewed insider's knowledge as a hindrance. "That's one thing I told people: 'Just because I know how it works internally doesn't make me the best player.' In fact, it tended to hurt me in a mental sense. It put me in a box. I know what it's supposed to be doing." Consequently, Arnold has only finished the game once.

Inquisitive by nature, Toy relied on planning and preparation more than any sword or spell.

> There's this taxonomy of video-game players. I'm an explorer. I tried on every piece of armor, drank every potion, read every scroll. I learned everything about everything that I could. At some point, you want to build up and say, 'Do I have a good sword? Do I have good armor? Do I have a scare-monster scroll?' You want a good set of tools. Once you've got that, you just run for it and hope you make it out in time.

Intellectual Property

Toy and Arnold probably would not have made much headway in converting the code they wrote at University of California. Glenn Wichman explained the unlikelihood of the game's original code making the leap to commercialization.

> When we wrote *Rogue*, we were students at the University of California, using the University of California's computers to create the program. *Rogue* wasn't our property. We really didn't have any legal claim to the source code. UNIX was distributed as source code to universities with the idea that they could improve upon it—ultimately what open-source ended up being.

A Bite of Forbidden Fruit

In 1982, Michael Toy and Ken Arnold traveled to Boston and gave a talk at USENIX, a conference dedicated to all things UNIX. Their talk centered on the benefit of letting employees cut loose by playing games at the workplace.

"The thesis of it was this: you can try and limit games—this was back when people used time-share—but the one thing your programmers are good at is solving and deeply understanding rule-based systems. If you come up with a system that forbids the playing of games, or removes games by looking for game files, they'll defeat it. That's what they're good at!" Arnold explained.

Arnold and Toy reasoned that it was better for managers to put a time limit on games rather than enforcing a prohibition. "It's kind of like alcohol and kids. You can tell them it's this forbidden thing, or you can give them a little and explain how it's stupid to over-drink," Arnold explained. Going further, Arnold and Toy pointed out that managers who tried to solve the problem of gaming at work by banning games probably weren't great managers.

Fundamentally, it doesn't matter if they're playing games or not. They're not doing work. You need to catch that and help them out of their hole in whatever way you think is appropriate. It's not about playing games in the workplace; people will find something else to distract them. Some people have no self-control.

The Copy Protection Mafia

To keep industrious players from hacking the game the way university students had at UC Santa Cruz and UC Berkeley, Lane added an anti-piracy tripwire humorous and lethal in equal measures. "The copy protection was a simple thing where something was written onto an unused track of the floppy disk, and if the game didn't find it, it assumed it was not the original disk it was shipped on," he explained.

If pirates triggered the tripwire Lane had planted on the disk, the monsters down in the dungeons dealt exponentially greater damage until players were inevitably squished. Cheaters were memorialized by an epitaph that read *Killed by: Copy Protection Mafia*. "It wasn't sophisticated, but that was in the days before hard disks, or at least they were too expensive and not very common."

Inked

In addition to drawing the sprites used in the Mac version of *Rogue*, Wichman submitted illustrations of monsters for the game's instruction booklet. "But Epyx didn't like my style, which, from my point of view, *Rogue* was tongue-and-cheek, so my monsters were silly looking. I liked them that way, but Epyx wanted to take it in a very serious direction [for marketing]."

[Editor's note: Epyx may not have seen eye-to-eye with Wichman on *Rogue*'s art style, but David L. Craddock, author of *Dungeon Hacks*, certainly did. Wichman was kind enough to create art for *Dungeon Hacks*.]

Black Magic

Many *Rogue* players have a leg up on Glenn Wichman. "I've actually never legitimately beaten the game. The only time I've beaten the game was taking advantage of a bug or playing in wizard mode." A debugging tool written by Toy and Wichman, wizard mode was a password used by *Rogue*'s original authors to quickly find and squelch bugs. "For example, a troll might be too powerful; things like that. We wanted to debug it, and we needed to quickly get down to troll territory without having to play through the whole game. So we put in this debug mode."

Wizard mode was the ultimate survivor's kit. Once activated, it gave players the ability to revive after death as well as create their own items. To keep players from using it to cheat, Toy and Wichman barred hacked characters from taking a seat at the top-10-scores table.

More Than a Pretty Face

Over the years since the roguelike genre's explosion in popularity among Internet users, many gamers have shunned color graphics, preferring the tried-and-true text-based graphics of yore. Wichman does not count himself among that crowd.

I preferred the graphics. I would have made it graphical from the beginning if the technology had been available to us. I think there is a nostalgic feeling to character graphics, and that was something I put back into the Atari ST version. In the Mac version, you could only play in graphics mode. When I did the Atari ST version, I put a classic mode in the preferences menu so you could go back to how it looked on the original UNIX machines.

Spice of Life

Before reuniting with Wichman, Arnold and Toy had experimented with ways to diversify *Rogue* even further. One idea was to randomize the player's stats every time they started a new character, but the idea fell flat when they observed players re-rolling characters until they hit on ideal stats.

Version 5.7, an update that Arnold and Toy were working on before they went their separate ways, would have introduced character classes. "In a role-playing game, if you're playing an elf, you act like an elf. But in a simple game like *Rogue*, you maybe have this special ability, but there's nothing really different about it [visually]. You could easily forget what class you were playing most of the time," Arnold explained.

Notes

1. *Rogue* made the cut: "History and Timeline." *UNIX.org*. http://www.unix.org/what_is_unix/history_timeline.html.
2. In 1965, Olivetti broke new ground: "Desk-Top Size Computer Is Being Sold by Olivetti for First Time in U.S." *Wall Street Journal*. http://bit.ly/1w43xyB.
3. As payment for the artwork used in the Macintosh version: "A Brief History of 'Rogue'." *Wichman. org*. http://www.wichman.org/roguehistory.html.
4. *PC World* put *Rogue* for the PC as the sixth best game: "The Ten Greatest PC Games Ever." *PC World*. http://www.pcworld.com/article/158850/best_pc_games.html#slide6.
5. Ritchie jocularly accused *Rogue*: "The Making of: Rogue." *Edge*. http://www.edge-online.com/features/making-rogue/.

4

There and Back Again
Retrieving the Sword of Fargoal

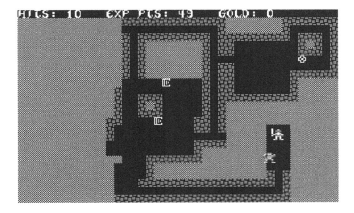

Sword of Fargoal running on a Commodore 64. (Image: Mobygames.com.)

Creative Encouragement

By 1979, desktop computers like the Apple II and Commodore VIC-20 were appearing in schools and businesses, and, on a smaller scale, on kitchen tables and in family dens. Managers and teachers still viewed computers as glorified adding machines and typewriters—tools that existed to increase productivity. Mike Seiler, a computer science and mathematics instructor at Henry Clay High School, was an exception to the rule.

"Much to his credit, he ended up allowing us to use the computer room during breaks and after school, even allowing us to have access to a key," recalled Jeff McCord, a student in Mr. Seiler's computer science course.[1] "It became clear that he recognized that making games was actually teaching us about the computer."

McCord's experience with computers predated his enrollment in Mr. Seiler's class. During his formative years, his father, Michael, taught computer science at University of Kentucky (UK). During Jeff's junior year of high school, his dad set up a student account for him in

UK's computer lab. McCord whiled away free time in the lab playing *Colossal Cave Adventure* on the Teletype (TTY), a typewriter-style terminal that printed game output on a gigantic roll of green-and-white paper instead of a screen.

"In *Adventure*, I'd get 200 lines ahead, and then I would die," McCord remembered. He quickly ran into the same problem that had soured Michael Toy on adventure games.

> The next time I played, I would type in all the answers because I had them memorized. I'd get 200 lines ahead and watch while the terminal cranked out paper. Eventually, I was able to solve *Adventure*, which was one of the seminal accomplishments of my formative years.

Beginning his senior year at Henry Clay High in 1980, McCord signed up for Mike Seiler's computer programming course. Seiler had recently convinced the school board to foot the bill for three Commodore Personal Electronic Transactor (PET) computers. Coming from TTYs and mainframes, McCord was floored by the PET. The nine-inch screen was couched in a plastic shell that also enclosed a keyboard, similar to a dumb terminal. But unlike a dumb terminal, the PET housed all the circuitry it needed to function independently from mainframes and minicomputers: a built-in cassette player for data storage, 4 kilobytes of memory, and a blazingly fast 1 megahertz processor.

Many teachers might have balked at the idea of turning juniors and seniors loose on $600 machines, but Seiler opted to keep his students on a long leash.[2] He enjoyed wandering around the room and peering over shoulders to see what students were working on, and lending a helping hand when they got stuck writing code. McCord rarely needed guidance. He was in his element. Wielding programming commands and a keen mind for logic, he wrote little games and showed them to Mr. Seiler and his classmates. His education in programming and game design continued at home. "My dad decided to buy a PET for home. Not only did we have ones at school, but up in the master bedroom's office area, I could go up and figure out how to program in BASIC."

Like most budding game programmers, McCord started small, creating adaptations of simple games like tic-tac-toe. After learning the commands and logic behind a game loop, the sequence of events that repeats until the player encounters a losing condition or quits, he wrote a version of *Othello*, a version of the popular board game *Reversi* where two players try to form unbroken lines of black or white discs.

While the PET allowed McCord to expand his creative horizons, it also put down speed bumps. His take on *Othello* required two human players; the PET's 4 kilobytes of memory were not enough to hold all the logic necessary to create a computer-controlled opponent. Better able to appreciate the machine's strengths and work around its weaknesses, he began work on his most ambitious game to date.

The Protectorate Sword

"I'd say there were about three or four key factors that helped me to get into that world of electronic versions of games," McCord explained. "One, of course, probably goes back to every designer's early gaming experiences: if they are at all interested in roguelikes and dungeon crawlers, they probably read Tolkien's books. And, of course, they played *Dungeons & Dragons*."

McCord was a self-professed super-fan of *D&D*. He bought the earliest edition of the pen-and-paper role-playing game when it hit stores in 1974. While his friends preferred to don armor and cast spells, he eagerly assumed the role of dungeon master, the storyteller in charge of guiding players on quests. Dungeon masters could stick to pre-constructed campaigns available in *D&D* rulebooks, or pen their own. McCord fell into the latter group. His grandest adventure centered on the Protectorate Sword, a blade sheathed in the stone floor of a temple that sat in the center of the Great Forestlands. Magical in nature, the sword erected a barrier that kept evil outside the forest.

Probing at the magical barrier, an evil wizard named Umla found a loophole. He cast a spell to disguise himself as an old man in need of adventurers to help restore peace to his homeland, and crossed the force field. At an opportune moment, Umla shed his disguise and absconded with the Protectorate Sword. The barrier came crashing down, and all manner of snarling beasts rushed in. Meanwhile, Umla erected a magical dungeon and descended to the deepest, darkest level, where he hid the sword away. The beleaguered inhabitants of the Forestlands sent out a plea for heroes brave enough to descend into the dungeon, retrieve the sword, and restore it to the temple.

To the delight of his friends, McCord ran his Protectorate Sword campaign for three years. When he was not sketching maps and the next chapter of his epic quest, McCord continued learning how to program on the Commodore PET in his parents' master bedroom. Constantly on the hunt for software, McCord hoarded issues of magazines like *BYTE*, *Creative Computing*, and *Compute! Magazine*, which published code for games. All an enterprising programmer had to do was type in magazine listings, weed through typos, and the game would materialize on the PET's screen.

Paging through a new issue, McCord hit on a code listing that covered the screen in a tangle of narrow, twisted passageways. Reading over the maze program, a wild idea occurred to him. "I remember typing the code into my computer and thinking, *Oh, wow. What if I could make this into an actual* D&D *game?*"

McCord embarked on a quest to convert his *D&D* campaign into a computer game, which he called *Gammaquest II*. "I probably did some sort of initial programming experiments that ended up being *Gammaquest I*," McCord told me when I asked about the obvious *II* in the game's title. "I don't know how the name came about."

Bookmarking the algorithm that generated twisty mazes, McCord set it aside. Such dense, tangled warrens should be reserved for something special, and he had just the thing in mind. In the meantime, he set about devising his own level-generation algorithms.

First, he would draw four or five rectangular rooms of various sizes and plop them randomly around the screen. Some might even overlap. Rooms were represented by colored blocks; black for flooring, white for walls. In the very center of each room, he planted two passageways, then let them unfurl. "The passage was like a little explorer; it would test ahead to see what type of block was in front of it. It would head out from a room and do random turns left and right and up and down—and eventually it would hit something."

Passageways stopped unfurling when they hit another room, guaranteeing that every room had two methods of ingress and egress. Somewhere in the level was a staircase leading down to the next dungeon. "What I like about random levels is that even if it's very simplistic in terms of visual representation, it lets the user experience their own quest, their own story, as the levels unveil themselves."

In *Gammaquest II*, levels unveiled slowly. Every level started out blanketed in green brume, which McCord referred to as the fog of war. As the player moved, the fog peeled back. Generating and peeling back the fog had required McCord to exercise technical wizardry. The PET had two banks of memory; one to hold the current contents of the screen, and a reserve bank to hold elements that the programmer did not want to display until they were manually moved over to the primary memory bank. McCord generated random levels in reserve memory first. As players moved, the game pulled from the fully constructed level held in reserve memory, revealing the level piece by piece on the screen.

Hidden by the fog were symbols that represented monsters and treasure. In contrast to the mainframes on which *Rogue* had been programmed, the PET sported a character set similar to ASCII. Called PETSCII (PET Standard Code of Information Interchange), the set included basic characters such as numbers, symbols, and upper and lowercase letters, as well as special symbols such as diamonds and spades, which McCord used to symbolize game elements.

Bumping into a monster—fantasy fare such as wolves, goblins, demons, and werebears—automatically initiated a scuffle, the outcome of which depended on how the player's stats stacked up against the monster's. "The game would look at the hit points and strength of the monster as basic characteristics, and those varied depending on the monster type." Monsters that lurked deeper in the dungeon had better stats in order to throw roadblocks in the paths of players who thought they could breeze through the game by rushing down to the Protectorate Sword and skirting encounters.

Automating combat was a decision McCord made purposefully. To him, *Gammaquest II* was about exploration first and foremost. He wanted players to feel like the authors of their own stories, focusing on where to go and what to do next. Getting stuck on tough enemies would have slowed down the narrative. To pull players deeper into their adventure, McCord added minimalistic text descriptions at the top of the screen. "Even if it's as simple as saying, *Treasure chest: 50 gold*, or *Powerful enemy* and then you would see the sounds of the fight, like, *CRUNCH*—that was forming a story thread."

Gammaquest II did not end at the sword level, the dungeon where the Protectorate Sword was kept, and a challenge deliberately unique from the ones prior to it. Ordinary levels consisted of wide hallways and rooms. The sword level was based on the maze-generator code that McCord had dog-eared in his computing magazine: a snarl of corridors that were too tight for players to dodge around the monsters guarding the legendary sword. McCord's major alteration to the code listing was to add a chamber in the center of the maze along with a contingent of nasty guards.

Rather than have the sword appear on the same dungeon every time, any level between 15 and 20 stood a chance of hosting the final maze. Setting foot in a new area only to see cramped corridors unraveling every which way never failed to send a shiver up players' spines. "I was excited to include something different, because you'd get there and recognize, 'Oh! I'm somewhere special!'"

Players had to work their way to the center of the maze to retrieve the sword. Once they did, they were in for a shock. Picking up the sword triggered a timer set to 32 minutes. Players had to rush back through the maze, up through the dungeons, and get to the surface before the timer expired. The return trip was complicated by the fact that hiking back up a staircase took players to brand new dungeons rather than the ones they had previously cleared. Generating new levels for the return trip was a decision McCord made based on technical limitations. "I had to keep it under 16K [kilobytes]. The entire game was about 14K."

McCord found the constraint frustrating. He had wanted to recycle old levels and repopulate them with tougher monsters on the way back up, but the lack of storage capacity, coupled with programming skills that had not yet ripened, prohibited him from saving the random number generated for each particular level, a seed that influenced how the level's design would turn out. He made the best of the situation by explaining away the constraint in the game's story.

> One thing that's kind of funny is, it's always possible, when someone can't achieve what they're after, to just explain it in the story. I remember deciding that the dungeon was magically created by Umla, so the dungeon changing [on the way back up] was not a big deal in my mind.

The *Sword of Fargoal*

By the end of 1980, McCord was still plugging away on *Gammaquest II*. He was still a regular in Mr. Seiler's computer courses, which allowed him to pick up on the game right where he had left off back at home. Classmates flocked to McCord's computer every time he premiered a new version. He listened carefully as they played.

> There were a bunch of friends who liked the game enough that they'd say, 'Oh, this is so cool. Why don't you consider doing an invisibility spell?' So I'd think, *Hmm, how would I do invisibility? Well, you would see yourself, but the monsters would just move around randomly.* Then they'd say, 'What about a teleport spell?' So I figured out how to do that. It all formed organically. It was something that kind of grew over time.

After graduating high school in 1981, McCord left his PET at home while he attended University of Tennessee, where he met a fellow Henry Clay High alumnus who shared his enthusiasm for computers. Whereas McCord had been raised on Commodore machines, this other student had grown up playing and making games on the Apple II. Most interesting to McCord, his new friend had written a game, sent it off to a publisher, and gotten a paycheck in return.

> I thought, *I have a game that's just sitting there.* I sent it off to the Library of Congress and got it copyrighted, and then I sent it off to about three or four different publishers, who were all pretty new at the time. One of those was Epyx.

Epyx was one of two publishers that expressed interest in McCord's game, but the only one to offer an advance. McCord accepted, cashed his $2000 check, and moved out to the San Francisco Bay Area, home of Silicon Valley and infinite opportunities made possible through technology. Per McCord's agreement with Epyx, he would maintain the copyright to his game and develop it for the Commodore VIC-20 and Commodore 64, the successors to the PET.

Working at Epyx's San Francisco office, he met with Susan Lee-Merrow, the producer assigned to him. McCord and Lee-Merrow knew they could not market the game as *Gammaquest II*, as the name implied a sequel to a previous title. McCord proposed changing the name to *Sword of Fargaol*. As *gaol* is a Middle English word that means *jail*, Lee-Merrow suggested a compromise. "She said, 'No, call it *Sword of Fargoal*. That's how people are going to read it anyway'," McCord remembered.

Since the VIC-20 was similar to the PET in terms of architecture, McCord converted *Sword of Fargoal* for that hardware first. Most of the underpinnings were carried over from *Gammaquest II*. The most obvious difference was the graphics. No longer reliant upon the PETSCII characters, McCord drew tiny sprites—two-dimensional images—to represent characters and items. The player avatar was represented as a knight.

Monsters got more than a facelift. In *Gammaquest II*, enemies had been straightforward: as players descended deeper, the monsters got more hit points and dealt more damage. In the VIC-20 version, they woke up when the player stepped within a certain radius of their location. From there, their behavior was binary. Some monsters roamed around randomly, while others caught the hero's scent and set off after him.

McCord put the VIC-20 version of *Sword of Fargoal* to bed and turned his attention toward the Commodore 64. Compared to the PET and VIC-20, the C64 was a huge leap forward. In spite of his best efforts to optimize the code, McCord was unfamiliar with the more advanced hardware, which caused certain operations to perform slowly. Like on the PET and VIC-20, he kept a complete version of the current level in reserve memory and revealed each floor tile as players explored. Unfortunately, the process of rendering the level piece by piece was sluggish, which made adventuring laborious.

The trouble, he realized, was that BASIC's simplicity dragged the game down. By comparison, assembly language was exponentially speedier. Unfortunately, McCord did not know assembly, but he knew guys who did. A friend of his, Scott Carter (now Corsaire), and a friend of Scott's named Steve Lepisto, were old hands at assembly. McCord convinced Epyx to bring them on so they could help him write *Sword of Fargoal* for the Commodore 64.

Arguably the most notable change to *Sword of Fargoal* on Commodore 64 was the sound. McCord had added simple beeps and chords to the VIC-20 version, but the C64 boasted the SID 6581 sound chip, which allowed programmers and musicians to create anything from beeps and chirps to full audio tracks and (admittedly muddled) voice playback.

McCord took full advantage of the SID 6581. He wanted to play short, trumpet-like trills that served as audial cues for triumphant events such as finding treasure and winning a battle. Writing a sequence of notes that rose in pitch, he broke the sequence apart and applied two-note sections to specific events. His most ingenious use of sound, however, was the chord he played for monster movement. Playing to the Commodore 64's brawnier hardware, McCord kept track of the number of steps players took as they moved around. After so many steps, the player-character would freeze, and the speakers would emit a low buzz that sounded like a growl. The sound indicated that monsters were moving around under cover of the fog. "I attribute that [sound effect] to an early experience. One of the first scary movies I saw was *Jaws*, with my dad. He took me when the movie came out, and you hear that, 'Dun-dun

… dun-dun, dun-dun-dun-dun.' That probably was the kernel of what led to the monster-movement sound."

McCord's sound effects heightened the trepidation and excitement players felt as they inched forward. Every time they heard the low, rattling growl, they were reminded that there were creatures actively hunting them, unseen beneath the thick layer of brume.

> When you play, you feel a sense of urgency. The sword has an importance to it. The fact that [the game is] so perilous, that you can die so easily if you're not careful, if you don't plan your journey, kind of all plays into that backstory, which is just silently there.

Epyx released *Sword of Fargoal* for the VIC-20 in 1982. The Commodore 64 version followed in 1983, the same year *Rogue* was released for the PC. *Sword of Fargoal* received praise straightaway. Johnny Wilson of *Computer Gaming World* lauded the graphics,[3] and *Ahoy!*, a magazine devoted to games for Commodore computers, commended the fun of adventuring through the unknown.[4] In 1996, the editors of *Computer Gaming World* listed the PC version of *Sword of Fargoal* at number 147 on their list of the "Top 150 Best Video Games of All Time."[5]

Back at home, people near and dear to McCord celebrated the release of *Sword of Fargoal*, too.

> Later, after my game was published, a younger friend of mine who was in Mr. Seiler's class brought a copy of the game to him. She described him exclaiming to the class about how I was a former student of his, and then almost immediately leaving the classroom, while in session, and walking briskly down to the office to show the game around to the staff.

Groundwork

Like *Beneath Apple Manor* and *Rogue*, *Sword of Fargoal* stands as an example of convergent evolution. Although *Rogue* was available across college computers three years prior to *Sword of Fargoal*'s commercial release, the PC version of *Rogue* was likely played by comparatively fewer consumers since *Fargoal*'s graphics and audio gave Epyx's marketing department more to work with.

Yet McCord prefers not to label *Sword of Fargoal* as anything other than an RPG. He had never heard of *Rogue* when he started writing *Gammaquest II* or *Sword of Fargoal*, just like Michael Toy, Glenn Wichman, and Ken Arnold had never heard of *Beneath Apple Manor* when they coded *Rogue*. Likewise, Don Worth had never met the *Rogue* trio.

Regardless, the influences and interests shared by the makers of *BAM*, *Rogue*, and *Sword of Fargoal* united them in spirit. More importantly, their games went on to inspire the next generation of designers eager to leave their fingerprints on the evolving state of RPGs.

*   *   *

Side Quests

(Turn to page 49 for Chapter 5)

All in the Family

Jeff McCord was not surprised when his passions for creative expression and technology conflated during his years at Henry Clay High. Art and science were in his blood. His father, Michael McCord, started out in University of Kentucky's mathematics department, then became a pioneer as one of the first professors in the school's new computer science department. Michael's interest was in natural language programming, a discipline that involved designing languages made up of commands closer to spoken language than computer code. "He used high-level programming languages like LISP and Prolog to produce what would become one if the world's leading natural language systems during the 1980s, and eventually moved to the private sector by going to IBM Research in Yorktown Heights, New York," McCord told me.

Any space in the McCord home not taken up by computers was covered in art equipment used by Jeff's mother, a printmaker.

> My mom had a studio in our house growing up. In fact, for her etching work, she always had an open tray—perhaps covered when not in use—of sulfuric acid to etch her plates. I remember our ceramic bathtub always having deep, etched rivulets into the glaze since she rinsed her plates in the tub. It seemed normal as a kid.

PEEKing and POKEing

McCord used the PEEK and POKE commands of the BASIC language to copy bits of levels from secondary to primary memory. PEEK allows a programmer to view the data stored at a particular address in memory, and a subsequent POKE manipulates the data at that address.

As the Commodore 64 and other 8-bit computers grew more popular, savvy players figured out that they could use PEEK and POKE to cheat. By loading the game into memory, players could freeze the program's execution, PEEK into memory to find the locations of values such as their character's life, strength, and gold, and POKE in new values that transformed their lowly avatars into god-like conquerors.

Automatic Convalescence

Even though *Gammaquest II*'s combat was automated, McCord added in several layers of strategy to keep players engaged. To regain life, wounded players simply stood in place. Being able to extricate themselves from a losing battle and convalesce in a corner depended on whether the player had provoked the fight.

"Let's say you were dealt a near-fatal blow," McCord explained.

> You could step away from the battle as long as you were the one who attacked. If you were not the one who attacked, you couldn't step back. You were stuck. That made it quite dramatic. You'd try to be the one in control, to make the first move.

Lost in a Maze

Over the course of following up with contacts to fill in blanks in my transcripts, I asked McCord if he could remember the magazine that had contained the code listing he'd modified to generate the final maze from which players had to escape in *Sword of Fargoal* (the rest of the maze-generation algorithms were his). He believed the code had come from issue #19 of *Compute!* published in December of 1981. As we both observed, the timeline didn't add up.

"What's really odd about this is that, with the date being December of 1981, this article would have come out a full year after when I would have likely been exposed to the maze-article I remember seeing," McCord wrote to me in an email. "It makes me wonder if *Compute!* may have printed a similar article before? Or did I see it from a different source?"

Making it even more unlikely that McCord had gleaned inspiration from *Computer!* issue #19 was the fact that it was published approximately 6 months after he had graduated, and almost 18 months after he had begun development of *Gammaquest II*, which became *Sword of Fargoal*, in Mike Seiler's programming class.[6]

Armed with dates, I scoured archive.org's catalog of scans of *Compute!* published from January 1980 through May 1981 in search of listings for maze-generation algorithms that he could have seen. I read the scans issue by issue, page by page, and turned up one likely candidate. *Compute!* issue #6, published in September/October 1980, featured an article written by a Joseph Budge that discussed how to draw a simple maze for use in a Minotaur game. The accompanying code details how to generate and update the maze as the player and Minotaur hunt each other. The catch: the code was written in Pascal, not BASIC, and the program was intended for the Apple II computer, not the PET.[7]

I ran the article by McCord, but it didn't jog his memory. I moved on to *BYTE* and *Creative Computing*, two other magazines that published code for the PET. Once again, I came up empty-handed. McCord mentioned again that the *Compute!* article from December 1981 looked most like the code he remembered extrapolating from.

Our fruitless search left both McCord and me frustrated and bemused. Ultimately, we agreed that a magazine listing had influenced his decision to try his hand at a maze game, but were unable to determine the magazine's title or issue in which the listing had been printed.

Capulets and Montagues

Back in the 1980s, fans of Apple II or the PET were like the Capulets and Montagues from Shakespeare's *Romeo and Juliet*, only without bloodshed. Computer enthusiasts picked a side, citing everything from esthetics to superior innards to justify their choice. While the PET's chassis housed a screen, internal components, keyboard, and Datasette, a port able to read software from cassette tapes, the Apple II was a LEGO-like assemblage of components. Apple owners had to connect the computer/keyboard deck to a television or buy a monitor separately, and the included floppy-disk drive sat beside the main deck.

 Storage was the most obvious difference between the warring tribes. Apple bundled one floppy drive with the Apple II, while the PET's all-in-one framework featured the Datasette. Cassettes were cheaper, but prone to breaking, and users had to rewind and fast-forward to get to the data they needed. In every other category, the two computers ran almost neck and neck. Both had 1 megahertz processors, 4 kilobytes of memory, and included permutations of the BASIC language so developers could start writing software immediately. In other ways, the PET edged out its competitor. Its keyboard featured over 20 extra keys, users could add memory via an expansion bay, and the PET cost $400 less.

Despite the PET's advantages, the Apple II came out on top in the United States. PET users could buy a floppy drive separately, but it was far from cheap. And although the Apple II initially had to be connected to a television screen for output, Wozniak had integrated color graphics technology into the machine. The PET's built-in display, while more convenient, showed only black-and-white images.

The main reason for the Apple II's success was the advertising muscle behind it. In the May 1977 issue of *BYTE*, Steve Wozniak, the engineer responsible for the design of the Apple I and Apple II, published an article extolling the Apple II's technical specs.[8] In a 1984 interview with an editor from *Byte*, Steve Wozniak reflected on the reasons for the Apple II's success.

> There were two main factors that led to our success—our floppy disk and *VisiCalc*. Out of the original home computers, which included the TRS-80 and the Commodore PET, ours was the only one that had enough memory to run *VisiCalc*. *VisiCalc* and the floppy disk sent this company into the number-one position.[9]

However, this story ends with a twist. Commodore did inevitably go bankrupt, while Apple has continued to thrive, chiefly by expanding its computer business to include MP3 players, smartphones, and tablets. But the Commodore 64 stands as the single, best-selling home computer of all time with over 22 million units sold.[10] Historians point to the Commodore 64's programmable SID sound chip—in addition to its colorful graphics, expandable hardware, and popularity overseas—as the primary contributors to the computer's success.[11]

Notes

1. Much to his credit: Interview with Jeff McCord. All quotes from Jeff McCord come from interviews conducted via phone, Skype, and email over 2012–2014.
2. Many teachers might have balked: "Commodore Introduces the PET (June 1977)." *Old-Computers. com*. http://www.old-computers.com/history/detail.asp?n=31&t=3. (Author's note: Commodore released the PET in June 1977. The original price was $495 for the model featuring four kilobytes of memory. After hundreds of orders rolled in, Commodore capitalized on the PET's growing popularity by bumping the price of the 4KB model up to $595. Mike Seiler got permission from the school board to equip his classroom with three PET computers three years after the machine's introduction, so I surmised that the machine's cost had already risen by then.)
3. Johnny Wilson, an editor at *Computer Gaming World*: "The Commodore Key." Computer Gaming World, *issue #11, July August 1993*. http://pdf.textfiles.com/zines/CGW/1983_0708_issue11.pdf.
4. *Ahoy!*, a magazine devoted to games for Commodore computers: "Vic Game Buyer's Guide." Ahoy!, *issue #3, March 1984*. https://archive.org/stream/Ahoy_Issue_03_1984-03_Ion_International_US#page/n47/mode/2up.
5. In 1996, *Computer Gaming World* listed: "150 Best Games of All Time." *CDAccess.com*. http://www.cdaccess.com/html/pc/150best.htm.
6. Making it even more unlikely that McCord (Side Quest #4): "Maze Generator." Compute! *magazine, issue #19*. https://archive.org/stream/1981-12-compute-magazine/Compute_Issue_019_1981_Dec#page/n55/mode/2up.

7. The catch: the code was written in Pascal, not BASIC: "Theseus Versus the Minotaur: PASCAL Visits Ancient Greece." *Compute! Magazine, issue #06.* https://archive.org/stream/1980-09-compute-magazine/Compute_Issue_006_1980_Sep_Oct#page/n63/mode/2up. (Author's note: This reference can be found in the Side Quest supplementary material for this chapter.)

8. In the May 1977 issue of *BYTE*: "System Description: The Apple-II." *BYTE Magazine, volume 2, number 5.* http://www.informationweek.com/systems/system-description-the-apple-ii-by-stephen-wozniak/d/d-id/1104356. (Author's note: This reference can be found in the Side Quest supplementary material for this chapter.)

9. There were two main factors that led to our success: "The Apple Story, Part 2." *BYTE Magazine, volume 10, number 01.* https://archive.org/details/byte-magazine-1985-01-rescan. (Author's note: This reference can be found in the Side Quest supplementary material for this chapter. Refer to the following link for Part 1 of the interview, which makes for a fascinating read: https://archive.org/details/byte-magazine-1984-12.)

10. But the Commodore 64 stands: "Timeline of Computer History." *Computer History Museum.* http://www.computerhistory.org/timeline2014/1982/ (Author's note: This reference can be found in the Side Quest supplementary material for this chapter.)

11. Historians point to the Commodore 64's: "10 Most Popular Computers in History." *How Stuff Works.* http://computer.howstuffworks.com/10-most-popular-computers-in-history.htm#page=10. (Author's note: This reference can be found in the Side Quest supplementary material for this chapter. Additional reference: http://www.commodore.ca/commodore-products/commodore-64-the-best-selling-computer-in-history/)

5

When the Inmates Run the Asylum
Hack-*ing at Lincoln-Sudbury High School*

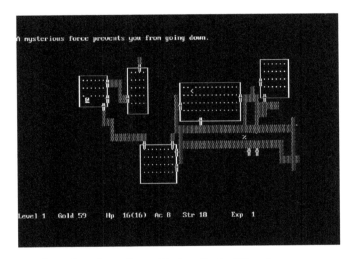

In most ways, *Hack* is esthetically similar to *Rogue*. (Image: HardcoreGaming101.net.)

No Official Status

In 1965, computer labs were just a stone's throw away in any direction at Massachusetts Institute of Technology. Most labs were identical in appearance: minicomputers that flashed and hummed while students retrieved paper from teletypewriters. Time-sharing had only recently been invented, but many computers only accommodated one user at a time, while others were punch-card behemoths, far too old to incorporate time-sharing technology. Most of the computers were owned by a research group and dedicated to specific tasks, rendering them unusable to students. A select few dumb terminals featuring screens were available, but always in short supply. A single PDP-1 sat in a corner, but was arbitrarily declared off-limits to first-semester freshmen.

Consequently, administrators monitored student usage closely. Students were given the bare minimum of permissions after logging in to an account, just enough to write papers and

49

conduct research. Brian Harvey, an undergrad pursuing his bachelor's in mathematics, found all the rules and regulations stifling. A single lab allowed students to work on unsanctioned projects, but first-semester freshmen were forbidden to cross its threshold; the Powers That Be worried that students would get caught up in hacking their own projects and let their grades slip.

None of that changed the fact that Harvey had a (semi-)legitimate reason for needing to use a computer. He was involved in WTBS, a student-run radio station, and had to maintain the mailing list. Another student understood his need and steered him in the direction of the Artificial Intelligence Lab, one of MIT's best-kept secrets.

For Harvey, working in the AI Lab was a breath of fresh air.

> When I found a bug in *TECO*, the text editor we used there, and brought it to one of the 'real' system programmers, he told me he was busy and I should fix it myself. He showed me how to find the source [code] and how to run the assembler, then I was on my own to sink or swim. I couldn't believe they'd let a freshman work on the real system programs. Especially one who'd just walked in the door, with no official status. But that's how it was: there was no official status.[1]

Students had the run of the AI Lab. They came and went as they pleased, and wrote code for any program that came to mind. When an official program sputtered, they rolled up their sleeves and dug into the code. Harvey carried the AI Lab's egalitarian spirit with him as he began his career in education and software engineering. Graduating from MIT in 1969, he went on to earn a master's in computer science at Stanford in 1975, where unrestricted labs like his safe haven at MIT also existed.

In 1979, Harvey applied for a job at Lincoln-Sudbury Regional High School (LS), a four-year public school in Sudbury, Massachusetts.[2] His official title was chair (and one and only member) of the computer department. Before his arrival, the computer lab had been a part of the mathematics department, but the installment of a separate computer division was proposed by the math instructors. They worried that tethering computer classes to their department would scare away students who might be interested in computers but intimidated by math.

All Hands on Deck

Before officially starting his tenure, Harvey talked to LS's principal, David Levington, about what he wanted to accomplish. "I didn't arrive with the complete vision of the structure we ended up with, but right away I talked the school into letting me not give grades, since I knew that would ruin the freewheeling atmosphere I wanted."

To Harvey's surprise, Levington was on board. Rather than hailing from education, Levington came from business, and putting a businessperson in charge of a school was usually a recipe for disaster: policy-oriented administrators often tried to micromanage even the most experienced teachers on their payroll, placing short-term goals ahead of long-term results. Levington defied convention; he made a habit of hiring the best educators for the job and then stayed out of their way.

For his next trick, Harvey needed to pull funding out of a hat. The school's computer, a PDP-8 run by the math department, was old and in need of replacing. Within his first few days at the school, the 8 crashed. Harvey, more familiar with PDP-10 hardware from his days in the AI Lab, had no idea how to restart it, so he asked a tech-savvy student to lend a hand. The student followed Harvey to the inner room of the computer lab, but hesitated, opting to stand in the doorway and shout instructions while Harvey fiddled with switches.

Frustrated, Harvey asked the student why he did not enter. The student replied that no students were allowed in the room because of the list of administrative passwords pinned to a wall. "That's stupid," Harvey remembered saying. He took down the list and declared that anybody with a valid reason for using the computers would be allowed access to the inner sanctum. For days afterwards, Harvey watched as students stepped into the room, looked around in wonder, then left without a word. "These tiny first steps already established my reputation as an educational radical—nothing about teaching or curriculum, just getting rid of stupid reminders to kids how little their wishes counted at school."

Harvey did not stop there. Writing a grant proposal to DEC, manufacturer of the popular PDP-11/70 minicomputer, he explained that he wanted to modernize his school's computer lab, but he needed DEC's help to do it. "What I really wanted was a PDP-10, the machine I'd used at MIT and at Stanford," Harvey explained.

> But I knew they weren't going to give me a half-million-dollar machine, so I asked for a free PDP-11/70, the most powerful model of their minicomputer line. In the end, they told me that DEC doesn't like to give 100-percent grants because then people ask for more than they need, but I could have 75 percent off of whatever I wanted.

Harvey petitioned the school committee to cover the remaining 25 percent of the funding. Levington went to bat for him. Money in hand, Harvey installed terminals all across LS: six in the computer center, a few in the library, and others in administrative offices where both teachers and students had access. Determined to give the kids hands-on experience, Harvey put them to work running RS-232 cables through the corridors, connecting each terminal to the PDP-11/70, which was stored in the lab's inner room.

Once the lab was up and running, Harvey invited his peers to drop by. Reactions ran the gamut.

> You'd open the door of the room and hear kids yelling across the room to their friends and project partners, see some kids playing games, some just hanging out, and others hard at work with total concentration. Teachers who thought that, in a proper classroom, every kid is doing the same thing at the same time, quietly, hated it. But other, more progressive teachers loved it. I was amused that every teacher loved or hated it *instantly*, the moment they walked in, without asking questions.

On most days, the computer lab was a disaster zone. The furniture became worn from students treating it like a trampoline. Sofa pillows were brandished in spur-of-the-moment duels. Computer paper littered desks and the floor. Larry Davidson, one of the math instructors, pitched an idea to Harvey: give the students the keys to the lab, allowing them unfettered access after school hours, provided they ran the space responsibly: set and enforce rules about reserving equipment, and pick up after themselves.

Placing a great deal of trust in his kids, Harvey handed the keys over. To his surprise, they devised a clean-up rotation where a different student was nominated to tidy up at the end of each school day.

Astonishingly, no damage ever befell any of the equipment. The terminals, printer, and PDP-11/70 were sacred.

The Computer Gang

Harvey continued running LS's computer center in an unorthodox way. Instead of cracking down, he offered more choice and responsibility. Early on, he charted a long series of courses that taught programming fundamentals and progressed to more complex lessons, culminating in an advanced programming course. He ended up trimming the curriculum to two courses: intro to computers, and advanced computer programming.

One aim of the intro course was to arm students with the knowledge they needed to use computers for other coursework, such as writing papers. Harvey's primary goal, however, was to teach students that they could make computers perform virtually any function imaginable by learning how to program. A filing cabinet in the computer center held worksheets that taught the basics of the Logo programming language and word-processing software. Early on, Harvey lectured one class per week and gave the students autonomy for the rest of the periods. Both Harvey and the kids ended up hating the lecture period, so he cut the lecture and simply made the rounds, answering questions and providing guidance when needed.

Harvey gave his students more time than there was work to be finished. Assignments had to be turned in by the end of the semester; if the kids chose to do work one day and spend the next day playing games, that was fine by him. The kids quickly discovered games like *Empire*, a multiplayer, turn-based strategy game. Most of the terminals were DEC VT100s, which presented output on a tiny black-and-white screen. The rest—claimed by students who had reserved them using a reservation system written by classmates—were DEC GIGIs, which displayed simple color graphics, perfect for computer games. "There weren't any commercial computer games back then. We had a copy of *Adventure*, and maybe a primitive *Star Trek* game, but all the rest were things we wrote ourselves. I remember one called *Bombs*, which involved being chased by monsters in a maze, and must've been one of the first real-time games ever written for UNIX," recalled Jay Fenlason, a former student of Harvey's.[3]

Harvey capitalized on the industriousness of students who wrote their own games. "I made game authors put their names and the school's name on the splash [intro] screen, so players would think, *This was written by a kid just like me*, and be inspired to learn how."

Students in the advanced programming curriculum had carte blanche. They chose what they wanted to make, and Harvey guided them along the way. Michael Thome, a student of Harvey's, was awed by the freedom Harvey extended to his students. Anytime Thome or his friends expressed interest in learning about new concepts, Harvey was on hand to encourage and support their learning. There was never any busy work because the students studied subjects that interested them. "By the time I graduated, I had several years of experience as a system administrator, had done UNIX kernel programing, had worked with robots, learned the basics of 3D graphics, and had built my own language—and the community was full of other students doing as or more advanced work of their own," Thome recounted.[4]

Thome was one in a gang of closely knit hacker friends. Jonathan Payne was another. A bookish prankster who spent his first two years at LS loitering in the library, Payne peeled magnetic strips out of books, planted them in other kids' backpacks, and doubled over laughing when they tripped the alarm heading out of the library. During his sophomore year, Payne started spending more time playing computer games on the terminals Harvey had installed in the library. Before long, Payne wandered into the computer center and became a mainstay. Excited by the student-first environment, he broadened his interests and wrote a popular take on *Emacs*, a text editor, which he called *JOVE*, short for *Jonathan's Own Version of Emacs*. *JOVE* grew popular enough to be distributed with the Berkeley-developed BSD UNIX operating system.

Michael Thome was one of Harvey's quietest students, and a good role model, if unwittingly so. When the other kids grew too rambunctious, Thome picked out a book, crawled up on a ledge near the top of one of the walls, sat cross-legged, and read. "He was very much part of the social group," Harvey explained.

> He was just more able to sit in one place and not be in the heat of every ephemeral activity. So he became sort of the stereotypical wise man of the group. Everyone looked up to him— me, too!—because he never yelled; he just always did the right thing calmly.

Jay Fenlason was one of Harvey's most ambitious students. Precocious and interested in nearly everything, Fenlason had a leg up on many of his peers, having discovered programming a couple of years earlier in junior high. "Programming was something I just fell in love with the first time I tried it. Here I had this powerful machine, and I could make it do anything that I could imagine. It was awesome."

Upon entering LS, Fenlason was one of many excited hackers who rushed through other work to maximize time spent in the computer center. "I don't really understand how any of the computer gang managed to pass their other classes," Harvey admitted wryly.

Fenlason divided his time between playing games and studying them. Of particular interest was *Rogue*.

> The summer between my sophomore and junior years, Brian [Harvey] invited some of us students to come out to California to [work as teacher's assistants during] a summer class he was teaching at San Francisco State University. While we were out there, we took a trip to UC Berkeley, where I got to play *Rogue* for the first time.

Fenlason had never played a game as immersive and complex as *Rogue*. After leaving Berkeley, he became driven to distraction by thoughts of questing down in the dungeons. Later in the week, he split from the group and hopped a bus back to the campus, where he invested more hours in the game. "I think I got a little bit obsessed then, and like any obsessed person who'd been cut off, I decided to build my own."

Reinventing the Wheel

Drawing on the eight or so hours he had spent playing *Rogue* at UCB, Fenlason laid groundwork in San Francisco. His intention, more or less, was to recreate *Rogue* as he remembered it: the dungeon layouts, the monsters, and the items. Fenlason dubbed his clone *Hack* for two reasons: "One definition was 'a quick [computer] hack because I don't have access to *Rogue*'. The other was 'hack-n-slash', a reference to one of the styles of playing *Dungeons and Dragons*."

Thus the roguelike, a game clearly inspired by *Rogue* rather than coincidentally exhibiting similar game systems and features, was born.

Fenlason composed a wish list of features he felt *Rogue* lacked, as well as those which *Rogue* could have implemented better. Level design, for instance, had been too simplistic; it would be more fun if players could explore dungeons that spanned more than a single screen. Monsters posed another shortcoming. There were only 26, one per capital letter—far fewer than the text symbols available. More egregious was that they all attacked in the same way, making a beeline for the player instead of, say, maneuvering around for a sneak attack or standing in place—perhaps blocking a doorway—and forcing the "@" avatar to venture closer.

"The most major philosophical difference I can think of is that I did not want to have limits imposed on what the character could do because of the interface," Fenlason explained. "So if your character is carrying 12 different kinds of potions and finds a new potion in the dungeon, they should be able to pick it up regardless of whether it is the same kind as the potions they are already carrying."

Other members of the computer gang—Thome, Payne, and another boy named Kenny Woodland—caught Fenlason's infectious enthusiasm. Like him, they simply wanted to reinvent the wheel and smooth out its rough spots. "Working on *Hack* was a matter of being able to add onto a growing game: adding features, fixing bugs, improving the performance—what every programmer enjoys," Thome explained. "I don't think the goal was ever really to clone *Rogue* as such, but to build a game that was satisfying in the same ways that *Rogue* was."

Playing the game was fun, but even more intriguing was its architecture. Curious as to how the game whipped up new levels every time he played, Fenlason hunted for source code so he could study algorithms that generated dungeons. It did not take long for him to get a prototype up and running. The earliest version of *Hack* was written in Logo for the Apple II, known as the Turtle Graphics language on that platform. Players could move their "@" around a screen devoid of floors, walls, and other dungeon decor. All monsters charged the player on sight.

Comfortable with the basics, Fenlason migrated to the C language, working on the terminals at LS connected to the PDP-11/70. As the game blossomed into a recognizable *Rogue*-like, he encouraged his friends to leave their fingerprints on his work. "Mike [Thome] came up with the idea of chameleons—monsters that could take on the appearance and abilities of other types of monsters," he recalled.

> Kenny [Woodland] contributed the maze-generating code for the bottom level that he and some other friends had written for *Bombs*. And Jonathan [Payne] and I had a friendly rivalry going on as to whose program, *JOVE* or *Hack*, could update the screen the most efficiently.

Community

In January 1982, Fenlason, Thome, and other students of Harvey's made the 40-minute drive to Boston to attend the annual USENIX conference, a confluence of hackers and a show floor where software developers and hardware manufacturers unveiled new technologies. By pure coincidence, Michael Toy and Ken Arnold were there to give a talk on *Rogue*, which the computer gang absorbed intently.

According to Thome, some of the students approached Toy and Arnold and asked for a favor. "The group of students ended up cornering one of them—I don't recall which one—and asked for the source code so we could fix the bugs/incompatibilities, but they politely refused."

Fenlason has no recollection of the conference, nor any meeting with Toy or Arnold. While Ken Arnold could not recall meeting any of the LS computer gang, he did remember several requests for *Rogue*'s source code.

> People would ask us, and we would turn them down. We thought we could figure out some way to turn [*Rogue*] into some cash. Remember that this was before the BSD license, GNU [a free operating system made up of free software] was pretty new and odd, and none of us involved had thought much about licensing and intellectual property issues. In retrospect, it would have been better to share.

Ultimately, Fenlason did not need *Rogue*'s source code. By the time he stepped away from *Hack*, he had managed to cross off nearly every item on his wish list. Only a few desirables had been left on the table. He could not figure out how to compose dungeons that took up more than one screen, nor could he figure out how to create pre-constructed levels that could be slipped into the stream of procedurally assembled dungeons. Innovations such as containers that could hold objects found during play, and light sources able to illuminate more than the floor tiles immediately adjacent to the player, also failed to make the cut.

Fenlason chalked up the omissions to finite hardware resources. "The limited address space on the PDP-11/70 severely constrained what I could do. I constantly had to trade off features I would like to see versus whether there was code space to actually implement them."

Hack was difficult to debug due to its inherent randomness. Many bugs occurred late in the game, but there was no guarantee that the algorithms would recreate the precise circumstances needed to pinpoint an error.

Before handing in his code, Fenlason made sure to give his friends, Thome, Payne, and Woodland, their due. "Really, Jay created *Hack*. Other kids contributed little bits. If you see names other than Jay's in the credits, it's because Jay really took in the lesson about not being possessive about one's creations," Harvey said.

Coincidentally, the completion of *Hack* aligned with Harvey's departure from LS.

> When a kid wanted to write a login simulator, I smiled benignly, thinking that that would be a minor activity. I grew up at the MIT AI Lab, where, back then, there was no such thing as passwords. I was certainly a hacker, in the original sense: I wanted to know how everything worked. But I had no curiosity about other people's secrets. So I underestimated how much energy the LS kids would put into password hacking.

The student who wrote the login simulator ended up opening Pandora's Box. During a day off, Harvey got a call from a colleague who was frantic over the state of the computer center: on three different occasions carried out by three different students, all on that same day, students had attempted to hack into other kids' accounts. Bowing under the onslaught of hacking attempts, the terminals had been rendered inoperable. "That was, I think, in 1980 or '81. And that's when I decided I was leaving."

Resolving to stay on until the school found a suitable replacement, Harvey spent the next year in a funk. He left in 1982, believing he had failed the students, the school, and himself.

However, two rays of sunshine cut through the gloom of Harvey's departure. The first took the form of lifelong friendships.

> I'm in touch with dozens of LS computer kids. This was probably the most intense time of my life. I felt part of a family in a way I've never felt before or since. My best friends in the world are mostly LS teachers and kids—former kids. I'm even friends with some of the kids' kids!

The second bright spot was that *Hack* stood and continues to stand as a monument to lessons learned in the spirit in which they were intended. Knowing that he lacked the time to patch in more features, Jay Fenlason arranged for others to build on *Hack*'s foundation. At USENIX conferences, hackers from all corners of the world submitted code on nine-track tapes, huge reels loaded into decks so their information could be fed into computers. Any interested members at USENIX could load a tape, comb through code, and make their own improvements. Fenlason thought *Hack* would make a fun diversion, so he copied it onto the LS tape—which also included Payne's *JOVE* program and dozens of other applications written by Harvey's students—and sent it in by mail.

At the top of *Hack*'s source code, Fenlason copyrighted it 1982 and wrote a note granting permission for anyone to modify and distribute the code provided his copyright remained intact.[5] His goal was to encourage others to learn from writing *Hack*, as he had, in order to preserve and spread knowledge.

Two years later, *Hack*'s code ended up in the hands of a hacker who took Fenlason up on his offer.

Notes

1. When I found a bug in *TECO*: Interview with Brian Harvey. All quotes from Brian Harvey come from interviews conducted via email over 2014.
2. In 1979, Harvey applied for a job at Lincoln-Sudbury Regional High School: "Brian Harvey." *Brian Harvey.* https://www.cs.berkeley.edu/~bh/.
3. There weren't any commercial computer games: Interview with Jay Fenlason. All quotes from Jay Fenlason come from interviews conducted via email over 2014.
4. By the time I graduated: Interview with Michael Thome. All quotes from Michael Thome come from interviews conducted via email over 2014.
5. At the top of *Hack*'s source code: "Hack copyright." *Hack.* http://homepages.cwi.nl/~aeb/games/hack/hack.html.

6

It Takes a Village
Raising NetHack

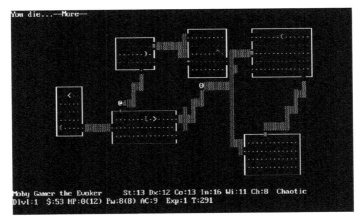

NetHack closely resembles *Rogue* and *Hack*, albeit with more color and deeper game systems. (Image: Mobygames.)

Hack + 1

Mathematisch Centrum was founded in the 1940s as Amsterdam's premiere destination for research in the fields of mathematics and computer science. During the 1980s, doctoral students, scientists, and postdocs scrambled to claim computer terminals so they could carry out their work in biology, cryptology, economics, information technology, and energy.

"During the daytime, there was a shortage of terminals, so game-playing was not done," explained Andries Brouwer, a mathematician and computer programmer in the department of mathematics at Mathematisch Centrum, known today as Centrum Wiskunde & Informatica (CWI).[1] When the sun went down and the labs cleared out, however, Brouwer moonlighted as the facility's resident game master. "The game master installed games, made sure they worked, and made sure the login that gave access to them was suitably restricted in time and capabilities."

According to Brouwer, CWI was one of the first facilities in Europe to receive Internet access. In 1984, while spelunking through the archives of businesses and universities that had gone online, he dug up the Lincoln-Sudbury tape submitted to the USENIX conference two years earlier. Sifting through its contents, he uncovered the *Hack* game made by the computer gang at Lincoln-Sudbury High.

Brouwer got hooked on the game and made sure it was installed on CWI's minicomputers, enabling other researchers to indulge in their proclivity for delving through dungeons. While his peers fought monsters and sought out artifacts, Brouwer observed their efforts with scholarly interest. "*Hack* was a topic [of conversation] near the coffee machine, and I also watched my brother play."

More interested in modifying the code than questing for loot, Brouwer listened carefully when players opined suggestions for new features. Being able to fight alongside pets was a popular request, so Brouwer added a few four-legged critters to the code. Fenlason had included 52 monsters in *Hack*, doubling *Rogue*'s bestiary. Brouwer added even more. Every addition broadened the options at the player's disposal.

> *Hack* became a challenge of a different type. Since there are many different things one might do, one almost always has the possibility to overcome a [challenge]. Just after one dies, one goes 'I should have...' and immediately starts the next game.

Traffic Jam

Brouwer eyed Usenet as the perfect distributor for his revised *Hack* game. Formed in 1980, Usenet functioned like a virtual bulletin board: users could post messages and files in various categories, called newsgroups, and other users could respond, forming chains of conversations and data. Unlike forums and bulletin board systems (BBS), which came several years later, Usenet did not utilize a central server to store and pass messages between computers. Instead, individual users managed newsgroups. As newsgroups made contact with other computers, they exchanged information, such as copying a message or file. Most newsgroups catered to a specific group of users. Fans of *Rogue* congregated at net.games.rogue to talk about and download the game, while net.games was a broader newsgroup dedicated to discussion about all sorts of games.

On December 17th, 1984, Brouwer uploaded *Hack 1.0* to the net.sources newsgroup, marking the game's first public release.[2] Stability was shaky on early Usenet connections, so Brouwer uploaded *Hack* 1.0 in 15 separate files for easier downloading. Over the following month, *Hack* 1.0 spread from news server to news server as more players caught wind of it.

Few, if any of the players who partook in *Hack* 1.0 were casual users. The Internet was still in its infancy, and years from being made widely available by providers such as America OnLine and CompuServe, who would bring Internet to millions of families around the world. In the early 1980s, anyone with Usenet access was a scientist, military personnel, a hacker, or a knowledgeable student connecting from a university lab.

Consequently, *Hack* 1.0's rapid spurt in popularity was driven by individuals with a keen interest in studying and sharing software, and who had a working knowledge of the UNIX operating system and software designed for it. "*Hack* was very accessible," Brouwer recalled. "Everybody could sit down and play. The movement commands ['h' for left, 'j' for down, 'k' for up, and 'l' for right] were identical to the cursor movement commands in the text editor, *vi*. Pressing '?' would give instructions."

As word of *Hack*'s breadth of gameplay spread across Usenet, more users stormed newsgroups in search of the game. Computers responsible for holding news posts and files buckled under the weight. In mid-January 1985, Gene Spafford, an avid Usenet explorer and professor of computer science at Purdue University, took the necessary steps to divert all *Hack* 1.0-related discussion and downloads to a central location.

> From: spaf@gatech.UUCP (Gene Spafford)
> Newsgroups: net.news.group, net.games, net.games.rogue,
> net.games.hack
> Subject: net.games.hack is created
> Date: Thu, 17-Jan-85 12:43:33 EST
> Date-Received: Fri, 18-Jan-85 10:15:10 EST
>
> There has been an incredible amount of traffic generated by users (and abusers) of the "hack" game recently posted to the net. I have just created the newsgroup "net.games.hack" for that traffic. Please stop posting articles about "hack" to "net.games" and "net.games. rogue" and use this new group instead.
>
> We now resume the disaster, already in progress.[3]

Brouwer did his best to feed the growing need for more *Hack*, rolling out new updates to the net.games.hack newsgroup. Version 1.0.3, released in July 1985, was three times as large as the previous version and included assorted new features such as the dog pet, shops randomly scattered throughout dungeons, and new monsters such as the long worm, represented on-screen by *W~~~~*. The long worm was one of many additions that required players to think strategically rather than simply confront monsters head on. Attacking the long worm's middle split it in half, creating two foes. To kill the creature without multiplying it, players had to dart around and attack its tail while avoiding its gnashing teeth. Other tactical considerations implemented by Brouwer included having to leave items behind when the player's backpack reached full capacity, and leaving space in the pack for gems and gold which increased the player's high score upon death. Players also had to forage for food to ward off starvation, which set in quicker as they grew stronger.

The 1.0.3 update boosted character diversity as well. Players could choose a class, such as the caveman (or cavewoman), and venture into new environments such as swamps, vaults, and Hell, the location of the Amulet of Yendor, which had made the jump from *Rogue* as the ultimate prize in *Hack*. Of course, players could not simply follow the linear path down to Hell, grab the Amulet, and celebrate. Adventurers who entered Hell without covering themselves from head to toe in fire-resistant gear were instantly burned to a crisp.

Curator

Brouwer moved on to other interests after releasing *Hack* 1.0.3. Like Jay Fenlason before him, Brower uploaded his source code, a torch passed on to anyone interested in carrying it. Another hacker, Don G. Kneller, stepped up. Kneller had gleaned hours of enjoyment playing the game on UNIX and decided to port *Hack* to Microsoft's MS-DOS operating system for PC. Carrying over the copyright license still intact from Jay Fenlason's upload of the game years before, Kneller called his version *PC HACK* 1.01e. He went on to release four more versions, each adding support for hardware such as the DEC Rainbow microcomputer. A developer by the name of R. Black downloaded *PC HACK* 3.51 and rewrote it in Lattice C, a permutation of the C language. Black then got the game up and running on the Atari ST, leading to the advent of *ST Hack* 1.03.[4]

Yet another hacker, Mike Stephenson, saw the merit in spreading the joy of *Hack* to as many hardware platforms as possible.

> I discovered *Hack* back in the '80s when I was working as an analyst at a computer hardware supplier and actually had free time on my hands. It was also just about the time I was discovering a variety of UNIX OS variants, [namely] AT&T and BSD, which were in a religious war at the time.[5]

Stephenson enjoyed the game but, like Brouwer, saw plenty of room for improvement. Using the 1.0.3 codebase as a foundation, he wrote patches that fixed bugs and added new features here and there. Other hackers were equally invested in growing the game. Izchak Miller, a philosophy professor who had lectured at Stanford and MIT, was teaching at University of Pennsylvania when he met Stephenson online in 1986. Janet Walz, programmer and avid *Hack* fan, was another early contributor. The three met over email and decided to collaborate on the code.

As the team grew, they began referring to themselves as the DevTeam. "I'm not sure when we started calling ourselves that, but I think it happened after we had reached a critical mass in the core of the team and had released at least one or two versions as a team," Stephenson recalled.

At first, the DevTeam focused on squelching bugs. It did not take long for Stephenson's team of hackers to penetrate *Hack*'s surface and make major alterations to its DNA.

> Eventually, the game had branched off from the original by a significant amount. Also, by that time, the core of the DevTeam had formed, and someone—I can't remember who, precisely—-suggested that we rename the variant that we'd created. I suggested the *NetHack* name [as a portmanteau of] 'UseNet' and '*Hack*.'

Released in July 1987, *NetHack* 1.3d was the first public release to distinguish *NetHack* as a separate entity from, rather than an update to, *Hack*. New features included weapons such as Excalibur, King Arthur Pendragon's legendary sword. Character classes derived from *Dungeons & Dragons* mainstays such as the fighter, elf, priest, and wizard were joined by the ninja, archeologist, samurai, and tourist, presenting unique alternatives for players who had grown weary of stereotypical fantasy fare. The tourist started out with lots of gold, a credit card, maps, and a camera able to be used offensively against monsters.

Although the DevTeam packed even more features into *NetHack* 1.4f, one convention of *Hack* remained constant. Players fought their way down from one floor to the next. The first 25 floors were standard dungeons consisting of rooms, usually rectangular in shape, chained together by hallways. Deeper down, the corridors narrowed and snarled, forming mazes. The ultimate goal remained to enter Hell and claim the Amulet of Yendor, which was in the clutches of a wizard camped out in the center of a fiery maze.

Four months later, the DevTeam rolled out another update, version 2.2a. New features included Medusa, the voluptuous she-serpent from Greek mythology able to turn adventurers to stone with a glance, and represented in *NetHack*'s dungeons by the number *8*. Twenty more dungeon levels were added, increasing the total to 60, but advancement to Hell remained linear.

Teamwork

In April 1988, the DevTeam patched *NetHack* to version 2.3e. The update introduced new monsters such as the giant eel and the Three Stooges of slapstick-comedy fame, appearing as @ symbols labeled *Larry*, *Curly*, or *Moe*, and as likely to smack each other as they were the player. New effects and implements were added. Eating the corpse of a slain quantum mechanics monster caused players to teleport around the dungeon at random. Magic wands could detect secret doors, spin monsters out of thin air, or polymorph them into a different species or object. "Special rooms" held treasure and dangerous enemies. One special room was the barracks, a large space filled with soldiers who stood a chance of being asleep, giving players a small window of time in which to ransack the place without rousing them.

Although *NetHack* 2.3e was the biggest version of the game yet, the adventure still boiled down to moving from Point A to Point Z. The DevTeam knew they needed more members to grow the game, and they did make the source code freely available on the *NetHack* newsgroup. However, they drew a fine line between users who downloaded the code and mucked around at home, and becoming an official member who made modifications that would be integrated into official releases. To join the ranks of the DevTeam, a programmer had to be passionate about ushering in change. Jean-Christophe Collet's desire to innovate fit the bill.

Like his predecessors, Collet gravitated to computer games after playing early adventures like *Zork* and *Wizardry*. In college, he studied UNIX and C programming, which led him to a vast repository of games.

> I got access to Usenet and discovered a whole bunch of games in source [code] form; the term open-source wasn't coined yet. Compiling them was rarely easy unless you had access to the same variant of UNIX that the developers of the game were using, but with patience and hard work, you could do it. It was also a great way to learn some of the tools and languages of the time.

Naturally, Collet found his way to *NetHack* newsgroups, where Stephenson and the DevTeam made source code freely available. "The *Hack/NetHack* source code was the way the games were initially released, which meant anybody could theoretically get them and port them to their computer—unlike *Rogue*, which required you to run [the game] on your institution's BSD VAX 11/780," explained a DevTeam member who asked for anonymity.

After uploading several rounds of patches, Collet caught Stephenson's attention and received an invitation to join the DevTeam. Collet signed on, and his name was added to the mailing list of developers who received every new snippet of code to test prior to public release. Collet's involvement in *NetHack*'s development almost landed him in hot water at work.

The company I was working for was paying for our Usenet access—not Internet; that was extremely rare in France back then—by the byte, so to speak. So when I joined the team, my mailbox started filling with huge chunks of code and patches, to the point that my boss pointed out to me that for that first month, my email traffic alone was nearly three-quarters of the bill.[6]

Worried that his situation might bar him from contributing, Collet explained the problem to Stephenson and the others. His teammates quickly concocted a workaround to accommodate him. Normally, each member of the DevTeam submitted patches through email. A proxy collected the patches and applied them to the main codebase. Due to his situation, Collet was given permission to code in relative isolation and send patches to another DevTeam member, who was in charge of making sure Collet's fixes stayed in tune with the collective. Every now and then, he received floppy disks via postal mail that contained code from the rest of the DevTeam, giving him the opportunity to follow their work.

Over the first several months of group development, DevTeam members filtered ideas through Stephenson. As time went on, he encouraged them to use each other as sounding boards, and to act unilaterally in most circumstances. "Little changes and bug fixes could just be put in unless somebody objected; larger ones should be discussed first," explained the anonymous developer. "Some things got voted on; some coalesced into The Right Thing; some were dropped when a strong objection [was raised] or several mild ones couldn't be satisfied."

Simply put, the DevTeam members were too busy with day jobs, and scattered pell-mell around the globe, to convene regularly. "I don't recall any big change that was made in the game by a person and someone else coded it. If you had an idea, it was not going anywhere [unless] you were willing to do the coding," confirmed Paul Winner, another DevTeam member. "It is also the case that some people specialized in certain aspects of the game. You wouldn't make changes to those areas of the game without talking about it with the appropriate person first."[7]

One of the earliest contributors to *NetHack* was Eric S. Raymond, a pioneer in the growing movement to support the distribution of source code so that others could learn from and build on software. For his first contribution, submitted in 1985, Raymond layered on a veneer of graphics by drawing dungeons out of solid gray bars rather than plain ASCII text characters such as hyphens and pipes ("|").

For his next trick, Raymond added vibrancy to *NetHack*. As of version 2.3e, some monsters still appeared in monochrome, while others were doused in shades of color. The use of color not only spiced up the game, but gave observant players more information to work with. Several types of dragons existed, and each dragon's breath dealt damage of a different type depending on the creature's color. Red dragons breathed fire, while blue dragons dealt cold damage. Players could file away the differences between each type and equip themselves appropriately before each encounter.

"This was about five years before color bitmap displays were common, which didn't happen until the early 1990s. The sight of color in a terminal window was actually startling then, even if you knew it was theoretically possible," Raymond explained to me.[8] Later, he added audio support, which manifested as beeps emitted from PC speakers.

Cult of Personality

While autonomy was the norm among the DevTeam, introducing a new character class required consensus. "I was a big fan of *Star Wars*, so I coded the Jedi class, adding things like light sabers, which required batteries to operate and you needed to replace them regularly," recalled Collet. "I had published the patch just before getting invited into the team, but it was deemed as a bit too far from the 'canon' [of *NetHack*]."

Designing character classes gave DevTeam members a chance to shine. Raymond had been the engineer behind *NetHack* 1.3d's tourist class, which offered an unorthodox play style compared to conventional fantasy archetypes like the fighter and wizard. Paul Winner modeled the barbarian after Conan, the popular fantasy character created by sword-and-sorcery fiction author Robert E. Howard. Winner researched the character extensively, going so far as to read all the *Conan* novels and take notes on the character's appearance and weaponry so that fans would recognize the similarities between the Cimmerian and their avatar's characteristics.

Winner pointed to the samurai class as his crowning achievement.

> [Creating a realistic samurai] meant adding quite a number of new things to the game, which I tried very, very hard to make accurate. Even references to the dog's name come from a Japanese dog that waited at a subway station for years for his master to come home, but the master had died.

DevTeam members who created a class were also in charge of designing a special quest for their class. Players who chose the barbarian had to journey through dangerous encampments of foes and defeat Thoth-Amon, a spell caster and nemesis to Conan the Barbarian. Character quests featured dialogue between non-player characters (NPCs) and the player-character printed to the screen. "The vocabulary used in the quest was very meticulously [written] to use formal speech. The reception that it received was rewarding," Winner remembered.

"We all had different backgrounds, therefore our references were quite varied. In the end, that diversity is reflected in the game," Collet recalled.

Quests specific to certain character classes were only some of the segues the DevTeam had in store for *NetHack*. Branching paths appeared in version 3.1.0, which Izchak Miller published to Usenet in 1993. One of the most popular paths was a staircase that stood a chance of materializing between dungeon levels 34 and 42. Trekking up the stairs led audacious adventurers to Vlad's Tower, a set of levels based on the legend of Vlad the Impaler, the historic figure who became the basis for Dracula. Players had to defeat Vlad to acquire the Candelabrum of Invocation, an artifact required to ascend, the ritual of handing the Amulet of Yendor to a god and completing the game.

"Let's be very clear: *NetHack* is a collaborative effort. I don't think there is a single feature, file, or anything, that hasn't been worked on by multiple members of the team at some point in time," Collet stressed.

> However, two contributions that I remember the most fondly are the special level compiler and Vlad's Tower. Creating the language and technology to script levels while remaining

true to the randomly generated part of the game has been one of the most rewarding challenges I've faced as a developer and designer. [Vlad's Tower] was often mentioned, much to my later delight, as one of the most devious parts of the game.

Every path added strata of exploration and gameplay possibilities, a feat made even more impressive by the fact that *NetHack*'s dungeons unraveled across a single screen. Confining level real estate to one screen kept the experience manageable for players, while adding dozens of branching paths—woven into the adventure via algorithms—breathed new life into each foray through the game.

"I believe Jay Fenlason's concept for *Hack*, which became *NetHack*, was just to build a better *Rogue*, and it never occurred to him to do otherwise," said Raymond. "Similarly, nobody in the *NetHack* group thought about the project as anything other than 'build a better *Hack*.' To everybody, this was *Rogue* with more features; why start from scratch when that concept worked so well?"

TDTTOE

Izchak Miller published version 3.0.0 of *NetHack* to the comp.sources.games newsgroup in July 1989. A moderator approved it shortly thereafter, marking the release as the first update credited to the DevTeam instead of a single contributor. Over the versions that followed, the gameplay became increasingly open-ended, enabling players to make their way through *NetHack*'s crucibles in any way they saw fit. Players could discard items onto a single tile of the dungeon floor, creating a pile, and then cast polymorph to transform every item in the pile into a different item. When players who journeyed with a feline companion opened a can, their pet would instantly appear by their side, an addition made by Paul Winner as a reference to his cats' uncanny ability to hear treats being served from virtually anywhere in his house.

Perhaps the most popular example of *NetHack*'s open-ended gameplay is the cockatrice, a monster able to turn players to stone by touching them. By wearing gloves, players can pick up a dead cockatrice and swing it like a club, petrifying any monster touched by the corpse.

The DevTeam's seemingly telepathic ability to predict every possible action gave rise to the acronym TDTTOE, *The DevTeam Thinks of Everything*. "The more options you have to manipulate the game environment, the more immersive and interesting the game is," asserted Raymond.

Another acronym, YASD, stands for *Yet Another Stupid Death*, referring to the countless ways in which *NetHack*'s algorithms can bring quests to an abrupt and violent halt. Some deaths, such as standing in the path of a fire-breathing dragon, seem prosaic compared to others that stem from innocuous actions. If players fall down a set of stairs while carrying a cockatrice, the corpse may touch their body, petrifying them. Knights, who attack while on horseback, stand a chance of slipping while trying to mount their steed, breaking their necks.

Over the years, such deaths have become known throughout the *NetHack* community as "gotcha" moments, deaths that occur suddenly and seem completely out of the hands of players. Some players do not mind them, while others call foul. The majority of the DevTeam believes they are part and parcel of playing the game. "*NetHack* tries to be an approximation of a real life experience," Stephenson explained.

> If you'd mounted a horse hundreds of times, you'd have patterned a 'mount' into your muscle memory and would execute it without really consciously thinking about it. Then, if something happened to go wrong—say, something slightly off with the horse's harness— oops! On your head you go. We do this via a random-number generation to try to simulate that sort of real-life set of risks.

"Players do have control over *whether* to mount the horse," pointed out DevTeam Member A. "Lots of things have both risk and reward, and if you find the risk too great, you can do something else instead."

YASDs have led some players to disparage the game, claiming one needs a detailed spoiler guide detailing the best equipment, the most efficient route down to the Amulet of Yendor, and which monsters to avoid at all costs, in order to win. Raymond believes the game has grown too arbitrary, the main reason he bowed out of contributing.

> There was a natural tendency for the devs to see the game from the point of view of some- one who played it constantly and obsessively; thus, over time, their notion of not making it 'too easy' gradually ratcheted up the difficulty level to the point where you couldn't really enjoy it casually anymore.

Thousands of fans, and more than a few members of the DevTeam, view the game differently. To them, *NetHack* is about the journey, not the destination—the same philosophy that guided Michael Toy and Glenn Wichman as they wrote early versions of *Rogue*. "You have to know a lot to win, but you don't have to know a lot to *play*, and we tried very hard to allow people to learn everything they need by playing—after initially reading the provided documentation. It took me years to win *Rogue*. I think I managed it one time. It was still fun without winning, and I believe *NetHack* is the same," explained an anonymous DevTeam member.

Paul Winner views death as a learning tool. If angry messages on Usenet excoriated a par- ticular trap, monster, or scenario, or if the developers themselves hit a brick wall, they weighed the merit of complaints.

> Things like starving to death and overeating are *designed* to make sure you learn to read the status [on the screen]. We didn't tell people they were feeling hungry in the beginning, so we did lighten up on some things, but in the end, you need to learn the game and gotcha moments almost always do that.

"Again, this has to do with balance," agreed Collet.

> The game is turn-based, so you can take your time and consider your next move. Most of the stupid deaths when I was playing [occurred] because I was [not paying attention]: hit- ting the move or attack key in sequence without too much consideration. That being said, I'm not saying that *all* these individual decisions are perfectly balanced, but overall, it seems to work.

Like most roguelikes, *NetHack* is viewed by fans and developers as extremely difficult. Figuring out how to conquer difficult dungeon levels, most of which will likely never be repeated thanks to algorithms, is what attracted developers and players to the game in the first place. "Many games seem to exist to be beaten and then forgotten—once you know how to do things, you can just do it the same way again and win again, so there's no point [in replaying them]," explained the anonymous developer.

"The aim of [*NetHack*] was to be difficult in the same way that an old-school *D&D* dungeon crawl was difficult, creating a strong sense of challenge and accomplishment," according to Raymond, who added that, for as capricious as *NetHack* can be, "I don't know that any of the other roguelikes managed this better."

Pioneers

NetHack has grown far beyond its origins as a cult game enjoyed only by hackers and college kids with Usenet access. In January 2000, *Salon* editor Wagner James Au crowned *NetHack* the best game ever.[9] "No graphics, no sound, no razzle-dazzle—but *NetHack* is still one of the finest gaming experiences the computing world has to offer."

Indeed, many designers of big-budget role-playing games lifted game mechanics from *NetHack* and gave them a graphical coat of paint. *Diablo*, arguably the most popular example of the hack-and-slash-style RPG, was the brainchild of David Brevik, who whiled away his college years playing *NetHack* and other roguelikes.

For members of the DevTeam, *NetHack* is a ticket to immortality. In April 1994, Izchak Miller succumbed to cancer. He was only 58 years old. Until the point when he grew too ill to continue, Miller, in addition to arbitrating code submissions and suggestions, had written the majority of the logic that controlled the shopkeepers that players interacted with over the course of their adventures. The DevTeam memorialized him in version 3.2 by inserting a new character named Izchak, proprietor of a lighting shop where players can purchase candles and lanterns.[10]

Besides gaining notoriety as the architects behind one of the most addictive and intricate games ever made, the earliest DevTeam colleagues are pioneers. At the advent of computers and for many years following, there was no difference between hardware and software. Programmers and administrators performed tasks on mainframes by flipping switches and pulling knobs. When commercial computers became available, companies began writing proprietary software that consumers could use but were forbidden to modify.

In answer, hackers around the world began advocating open-source software during the 1980s. Eric S. Raymond of the *NetHack* DevTeam is one of the leaders of the open-source movement. Raymond authored "The Cathedral and the Bazaar," an essay later expanded into a book in which he espouses that open-source software is technically superior to proprietary software.[11] The more programmers able to evaluate code, Raymond argues, the faster bugs can be expunged and updates pushed out.

Stephenson believes that *NetHack* played a part in the open-source movement.

> We pre-dated open-source [as a formalized movement], but I do think that the fact that we made a huge amount of source code available, without charge and under a public license—an early variant of the LGPL [Lesser General Public License]—helped to promote the idea of making software available for public use without cost. I think the other thing that really contributed to the concept of open-source is that *NetHack* has, and still does, accepted bug reports and feature ideas from anyone.

In December 2003, the DevTeam released version 3.4.3 of *NetHack*. The update marked the 29th public release of the game—and, as of this printing, the most recent release. Regardless of its long dormancy, *NetHack* is proof that compelling gameplay, not state-of-the-art graphics, stand the test of time.

"I am, to this day, incredibly proud of having been part of this adventure," Collet told me. "The fact that almost 30 years later I'm still answering questions about it, and that it is still seen as such a reference, never ceases to amaze me. The friends I made during that time are some of the most precious people in my life, and I'm so grateful that I was so incredibly lucky."

*   *   *

Side Quests

(Turn to page 71 for Chapter 7)

Missing Data

Today, users are accustomed to downloading games measured in gigabytes. Even the largest download can be completed in less than an hour, depending on the speed of the user's connection and the servers on which the game is stored.

When Andries Brouwer released his *Hack 1.0* update in December 1984, the game was packaged in 15 separate files totaling 400 kilobytes in size—small enough to fit on a floppy disk three times over. Yet newsgroups that hosted the game could not handle more than a few users downloading the game at once. To reduce the total size of the download, Brouwer released *Hack 1.0.1* as an update that required a separate file called "patch" to run. Unfortunately, not every site had access to the patch file.

Brouwer devised a clever workaround to the file-size and traffic problems. Once again he rolled out a fresh copy of the source code distributed among separate files, but released each on a different day. "In the coming two weeks I'll distribute Hack version 1.0.2 (10 parts, one 45K part each working day); the first part is posted today," Brouwer announced in a message posted to net.games.hack on April 1st, 1985.[12] "Contrary to Hack 1.0 which is a very stable program […] this new release is virtually untried, and may be full of bugs."

Over time, bugs turned out to be the least of Brouwer's problems with *Hack 1.0.2*. All ten parts made their way to the *Hack* newsgroup, but the second part became lost as years passed. Brouwer had released version 1.0.3 in late July of 1985, but became interested in tracking

down the missing file from 1.0.2 purely out of curiosity. More than 20 years later, it finally
turned up.

> Subject: Lost Part 2 of Hack 1.0.2 found
> Date: Fri, 9 Sep 2005 21:52:34 +0000
>
> An almost complete distribution of Hack 1.0.2, including Part 2 (which is missing from
> Google), has turned up at: http://vmsone.com/~decuslib/unixsig/uni87a/hack/[13]

The message came from a *Hack* player named Ray Chason, who wrote to Brouwer to share
the good news. Brouwer repackaged 1.0.2 for posterity; you can find it at http://homepages.
cwi.nl/~aeb/games/hack/hack.html.

Man's Best Friend

Editor's note: Paul Winner's samurai quest involving a dog waiting for its master is likely in
reference to Hachikō, the faithful companion of University of Tokyo professor Hidesaburō
Ueno.[14] Each day the professor and his dog walked to and from Shibuya Station. For nine years
after Ueno's death, Hachikō returned to Shibuya Station to await his master.

Hachikō—often referred to as chūken Hachikō (faithful dog Hachikō)—is immortalized
at the modern Shibuya Station with a bronze statue and a yearly remembrance ceremony on
April 8.

Notes

1. During the daytime, there was a shortage of terminals: Interview with Andries Brouwer. All quotes
   from Andries Brouwer come from interviews conducted via email over 2014.
2. On December 17, 1984: "Hack and copyright." *Hack.* http://homepages.cwi.nl/~aeb/games/
   hack/hack.html.
3. From : spaf@gatech.UUCP: Ibid.
4. Author's note: From this point on in the chapter, I refrained from citing dates on which updates to
   Hack and *NetHack* were released, since they can all be found on the *NetHack* Wikia's history page:
   http://nethack.wikia.com/wiki/Game_history.
5. I discovered *Hack* back in the '80s: Interview with Mike Stephenson. All quotes from Mike
   Stephenson come from interviews conducted via email over 2014.
6. The company I was working for was paying for our Usenet access: Interview with Jean-Christophe
   Collet. All quotes from Jean-Christophe Collet come from interviews conducted via email over
   2014.
7. I don't recall any big change: Interview with Paul Winner. All quotes from Paul Winner come from
   interviews conducted via email over 2014.
8. This was about five years before color bitmap displays: Interview with Eric S. Raymond. All quotes
   from Eric S. Raymond come from interviews conducted via email over 2014.
9. In January 2000, *Salon* editor James au Wagner: "The best game ever." *Salon.* http://www.salon.
   com/2000/01/27/nethack/.
10. The DevTeam memorialized him in version 3.2: "Izchak Miller." *Wikia.* http://nethack.wikia.
    com/wiki/Izchak_Miller.
11. Raymond authored "The Cathedral and the Bazaar,": Author's note: Raymond's book is a moving
    target, and he gives all interested parties access to "almost all" of its contents on his website, http://
    www.catb.org/esr/writings/cathedral-bazaar/.

12. In the coming two weeks: "1.0.2 announced." *Hack*. http://homepages.cwi.nl/~aeb/games/ hack/1.0.2-announced. (Author's note: This reference can be found in the Side Quest supplementary material for this chapter.)

13. Subject: Lost Part 2 of Hack 1.0.2 found: "Hack and copyright." *Hack*. http://homepages.cwi. nl/~aeb/games/hack/hack.html. (Author's note: This reference can be found in the Side Quest supplementary material for this chapter.)

14. Paul Winner's samurai quest involving a dog waiting: "Canine Imperialism." *Berfrois*. http://www. berfrois.com/2011/09/aaron-herald-skabelund-hachiko/ (Author's note: This reference can be found in the Side Quest supplementary material for this chapter.)

7

None Shall Pass
Braving the Mines of Moria

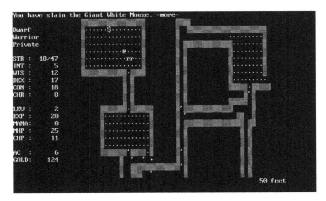

Moria's levels stretch across several screens. Here, you can see hallways running off the edges of the screen. (Image: Mobygames.)

> I have heard that there are still forgotten treasures of old to be found in the deserted caverns of the mines of Moria, since the dwarf and goblin war.
>
> —Elrond, Lord of Rivendell[1]

Robert Koeneke was a worthless degenerate—or at least, the principal of Putnam City West High School in Bethany, Oklahoma, seemed to think so. Koeneke had long hair, and worse still, his teachers reported that he never so much as cracked a book or turned in homework. No doubt he was just another hippie who wasted his life sleeping in class and getting high.

Koeneke's principal had him all wrong. He never used drugs. True, he rarely read his textbooks, but he earned high marks in his courses. He was particularly fluent in math and science. As a matter of fact, lots of subjects intrigued him. He simply preferred to approach education the way he approached everything else: at his leisure.

One afternoon in 1973, Koeneke's math teacher gathered the class and walked them down the hall to the principal's outer office. There, Koeneke beheld a strange box sitting next to a telephone receiver. The teacher identified the box as a computer, and the receiver as an acoustic coupler connected to a 110-baud modem. When users dialed a number, the computer emitted a high-pitched whining noise. Users then placed the receiver into a set of rubber cups, and waited for the terminal to beep back. A string of text characters, a human-readable translation of the drones and crackles emitted by the modem, appeared on the screen. Users could type responses, which the terminal translated into sounds and sent back through the modem.

Koeneke was unimpressed. He could not think of any reason to communicate with a machine in a language that consisted of shrill whines. Then, wandering the halls one evening after school had let out, he heard laughter and applause coming from the principal's office. "I investigated, and found a small crowd of students playing on the computer," Koeneke recalled. "It was a football game, where the Creampuffs, the user's team, played against the computer's team. I was fascinated! Soon, I began coming in late every evening and playing computer games."[2]

Although loitering to play games did nothing to smooth over his reputation with the administration, Koeneke did more than play. He began to wonder what made games tick. While rooting around the room for diskettes one evening, he found a thick booklet titled *BASIC Reference Manual*.

> Soon, I was programming in BASIC and discovered something even more rewarding than playing a game: writing one. Later that year, I managed to get hold of a green manual called *FORTRAN IV Reference Manual* and taught myself FORTRAN.[3]

Koeneke graduated from high school a year early in 1975. That same year, he enrolled at University of Oklahoma. Giddy at the prospect of absorbing all that higher education had to offer, he sampled major after major until he landed on electrical engineering, a discipline that gave him endless opportunities to flex his creativity and penchant for logic problems.

He sequestered himself in the engineering department's computer lab and claimed a dumb terminal, which displayed early versions of UNIX sent through the PDP-11/70 minicomputer chugging away in the basement. The lab's administrators, much looser than the draconian principal at his old high school, extended an open invitation to stay over and play computer games they had downloaded from other colleges and facilities.

Nosing around, Koeneke unearthed *Colossal Cave Adventure*. Like many other roguelike pioneers, he became hooked on the game and spent many evenings spelunking virtual caves. Inspired, he sat down at a Radio Shack TRS-80 personal computer—one of the competitors to the Apple II and Commodore PET—and wrote his own text adventure called *Pyramid*. The goal was to explore an Egyptian tomb and arrive at the treasure chamber in the heart of the maze. To impede the player's progress, Koeneke stationed monsters around the pyramid. Each foe was stationed in a specific room and unable to wander the maze freely.

After finishing *Pyramid*, Koeneke set the game aside and immediately wrote another. Each game was more sophisticated than the last, and was influenced by what he was playing in the engineering lab at the time. Around 1981, Koeneke found an early version of *Rogue* written by Michael Toy and Glenn Wichman. The hours he had spent exploring *Colossal Cave Adventure* paled in comparison to his obsession with *Rogue*.

> I guess what fascinated me about *Rogue* was how many different things you could find, and when you found stuff, you didn't know what it was. That was a new concept. Also, you could run through the game and play different dungeons every time. That was cool.[4]

To Koeneke's dismay, a threat more fearsome than the 'T' that stood for troll rose up and blocked access to his games.

> hey [administrators from the engineering department] decided people were wasting too much time at night and on the weekends, so they made a rule that they were shutting down game access. The systems administrators could still get to them, but if you weren't one of them, you were just out of luck.

Koeneke seethed. Playing and programming games had taught him more about computers than his textbooks and lectures. Suddenly, a flash of creativity cooled his anger. If he couldn't play *Rogue*, he would just write a version of his own.

Shortly after he discovered *Rogue*, Koeneke got a job on campus as an assistant in the university's computer department, where he was in charge of running the math department's minicomputer. The work was born of necessity. He had blown through a four-year scholarship bouncing between majors and, now on the computer science track, had to fund his part-time schooling out of his own pocket. His job was to help students struggling with computer-oriented assignments on the VAX 11/780. The prohibition on games had not followed him from the engineering department, but there were no games available for the VAX. That, he decided, was a problem that demanded a solution.

Suffering from a severe case of *Rogue* withdrawal, Koeneke decided to fill the minicomputer's blank slate with his dungeon hack. For the most part, he would stick to *Rogue*'s trappings: procedurally generated dungeons, a trove of artifacts and items to find, and monsters to kill, all wrapped in a text-generated package. Unlike *Rogue*, however, his game would take place in an established setting.

> I'm a big Tolkien fan. I'd probably read *Lord of the Rings* at least 10 times before I wrote my game. Of course, I also played dungeon master in our *D&D* games. I ran [players] through the Mines of Moria. I thought it would be cool to go down into a sophisticated dungeon, which the Mines of Moria were, and fight a Balrog.

> *All about them as they lay hung the darkness, hollow and immense, and they were oppressed by the loneliness and vastness of the delven halls and endlessly branching stairs and passages. The wildest imaginings that dark rumour had ever suggested to the hobbits fell short of the actual dread and wonder of Moria.*[5]

The Mines of Moria—words that struck terror in the hearts of the many races that inhabited Tolkien's classic fantasy epic. Located deep beneath the Misty Mountains, Moria was a subterranean city that spanned countless chambers, great halls, and tunnels. Each floor descended deeper beneath the earth. Orcs and goblins infested the mines until tribes of dwarves led by King Durin VI entered the caverns and routed the scourge. Making themselves at home, King Durin's band rechristened the halls Khazad-dûm, dwarvish for "the Delving of the Dwarves." Smiths fired up their furnaces while their brethren dug deeper in search of riches. Archivists documented their king's colonization of the underground city. For a while, the dwarves were content, working and digging and amassing great wealth.

Then the explorers awoke something in the dark: a Balrog, a demonic creature that towered over the dwarves and wrapped itself in fire and darkness. The dwarves assembled armies, but they were no match for the Balrog. The monster cut down King Durin VI in one early battle, earning it the name Durin's Bane. Orcs and goblins took advantage of the chaos and returned to the halls. Outnumbered, the surviving dwarves fled Khazad-dûm, forfeiting the bodies of their fallen kin, the weapons they had wielded in battle, and the treasures they had salvaged.

> 'We have barred the gates, but cannot hold them for long. We cannot get out. They have taken the Bridge and the Second Hall. We cannot get out. The end comes. Drums, drums in the deep. They are coming.'—An entry from The Book of Mazarbul, written by Ori and recovered in the Mines of Moria[6]

Once filled with the sounds of ringing hammers and roaring flames, Moria grew cold and dark. Elves and other races steered clear, calling it "the Black Pit." Goblins, orcs, and other horrors remained, beating their drums in the dark and cutting down adventurers drawn by rumors of abandoned riches. In the deepest recesses of the mines, Durin's Bane slumbered.

Koeneke aimed to wake it up.

Early on, Koeneke's goal for *Moria* was simple: recreate *Rogue* in an iconic setting that captured the thrills associated with another of his favorite hobbies.

> I'm a spelunker. When I'm in a cave, I feel the excitement of wanting to find out what's around the next corner. I wanted players to feel like there were no boundaries [in *Moria*]. There's always something around the next corner. I also wanted players to feel a feeling of suspense: 'When I open this door, what's going to come get me?'

Breaking ground in 1981, Koeneke built on the foundations of *Rogue*: procedurally generated dungeons drawn with text-based characters, monsters represented by capital letters, and an "@" avatar controlled by the player.[7] Then he began adding items. Since he had no way to consult *Rogue*'s catalog—the game was stored on the PDP-11/70 back in the engineering lab, where the administrators lorded over games—he wracked his brain to remember items he had discovered during his adventures, then expanded, consulting *Dungeons & Dragons* manuals and his imagination for ideas for new treasures. His goal was for players to find treasures every time they played, never coming across the same item twice. He also viewed *Rogue*'s dungeon cap, 26 floors at most, as too short, and set the maximum to 50, a number that could be changed by tinkering in the game's data.

Movement was another area of *Rogue* Koeneke believed was in need of a drastic overhaul. Toy and Wichman had mapped movement to H, J, K, and L—up, down, left, and right, respectively—the same keys used to move the cursor in *vi*, the word processor packaged with BSD UNIX. Those keys were familiar to college students who used *vi*, but not casual users. More problematic was the fact that *Rogue* used virtually every key on the keyboard to perform actions—quaff potions, rest, open inventory, test for traps, and loads more—which overwhelmed new players.

Facilitating intuitive movement in *Moria* would be easy, Koeneke realized. *Rogue* had been developed on terminals that lacked arrow keys, the natural choice for movement in games. Koeneke was writing *Moria* on a Teleray-10 terminal, which included numeric keypads, so he mapped movement to the 8, 2, 4, and 6 keys, which doubled as up, down, left, and right arrows, respectively.

Koeneke completed work on his early versions of *Moria*, which he dubbed the 0.x versions. After taking each update through a trial run, he grew discouraged. *Moria* was just *Rogue* with more items and levels. By attempting to recreate *Rogue*, he had inherited what he perceived as its limitations. Each of his levels was still a nine-by-nine array of rooms that fit on a single screen. Single-screen dungeons failed to capture the foreboding atmosphere and staggering enormity of the Mines of Moria. He wanted circuitous passages and dungeons that spilled over two, three, even four screens, so players could become lost and frightened. Successfully traversing massive dungeons would heighten the already-exuberant feeling of finding some new trinket or weapon down in the darkest depths, where truly terrifying foes lay in wait.

Koeneke decided to let *Moria* simmer on the backburner while he worked on other projects. As time passed, his brain ticked away, mapping out a complete overhaul of *Rogue*. The prospect of improving on *Rogue* was as daunting as it was exciting. "The most challenging part was the fact I'd never seen a program behave the way I was trying to make mine behave," Koeneke explained.

> It wasn't so much doing it; it was figuring out what I wanted to do. That sounds weird, but it was kind of a creative thing. For example, I'd never seen a game that shifted the screen, and I'd never seen a game where you would build dungeons randomly. And line of sight? Oh my god. How do you [determine what the player] can see in a very, very efficient manner?

By March 1983, *Moria* had lain fallow for nearly a year. Two major life changes spurred Koeneke to return to the dwarven city. The first was that he had become engaged to Debra Jean Lee, a medical technology major who had been hanging around the computer lab. Koeneke was head over heels in love, but equally terrified by the notion of settling down and providing for a family. The second major event was that he signed up for an operating systems course that required knowledge of PASCAL, a language unknown to him.

That summer, he resolved to get a jump on the upcoming class: he would learn PASCAL by rewriting *Moria* in the language. Not only would that help divert his attention from the pressure of his upcoming nuptials, but it would give him the opportunity to learn something new. *Moria*'s 0.x versions had been written in BASIC, which was intended for designing smaller programs. To make his game bigger, he needed more power and flexibility. PASCAL gave him both, chiefly through data structures.

In programming, a data structure is a container able to hold several different pieces of related data. A structure labeled *monster*, for instance, may contain data that defines how much damage a monster inflicts, how many life points it has, and its name. The programmer can then derive many different enemies from the *monster* structure, such as zombie, dragon, troll, and Balrog, and set each monster's particular data: zombies get 10 life points and deal between 2 and 5 damage, Balrogs get 5000 life points and deal exponentially more damage, and so on.

Data structures made Koeneke giddy with excitement. Anytime he thought of a new monster, he could simply derive it from his basic *monster* structure. "Everything was data driven. What that meant was amazing flexibility. You didn't spend all your time coding. You spent more and more time being creative."

Unlike its predecessors, *Moria* was built from the ground up to be a real-time game: instead of monsters and players alternating between turns, Koeneke commanded them to move according to set movement speeds. His play testers ended up hating the game; due to the complexity of *Moria*'s rules and systems, they preferred to take their time and think each move through, rather than be harried by attackers able to move around freely. Koeneke mollified them by converting the game to a turn-based paradigm.

Coding dungeons that stretched over several screens was a trickier endeavor. Koeneke's solution was elegant.

> What I did was I created a virtual view, a window, over a large dungeon. You only saw part of the dungeon at any given time. Given the computer resources we had back then, it was very crude; [the window] shifted by a quarter screen. But I'd never seen a game do that.

Like the dungeon level cap, the size of dungeons was configurable in *Moria*'s data.

> You could pick the dungeon height and width, the size of the view port, and how much it slid when necessary to keep the player on the screen. I played around with sliding one column at a time—a smooth slide like modern games—but it just required too much resources and was not efficient for running lots of players simultaneously.

As the game took on more features, Koeneke invited players to test-drive *Moria*. When dozens of students sat down to terminals connected to the VAX, the game slowed to a crawl. Koeneke quickly figured out why. "When there were lots of players on, and each dungeon had 30 or 40 monsters running around, the computer would just grind to a halt. There were too many requests [sent to the VAX] to compute mathematical problems."

Koeneke pinpointed the hefty calculations needed to determine line of sight as the culprit. Complex viewing angles, such as a player rounding a bend and spotting a monster standing in a doorway catty-corner to his position, squeezed more power from the VAX. More players meant the minicomputer had to work harder to fulfill every computation. No matter how Koeneke crunched the numbers, *Moria* still ran inefficiently.

One night, Koeneke's friend and boss pried him away from the computer and convinced him to have a few drinks at a nearby bar. The break turned out to be exactly what Koeneke needed.

> We had about three or four pitchers of beer. And while we were sitting there, I just had this epiphany. It just struck me like lightning. So I hurried back to OU. It was two in the morning. I got into my office and coded that stupid thing before I forgot how to do it.

Koeneke dragged himself back to the lab late the next morning and pulled up his code, afraid that his booze-addled brain might have done more harm than good. His bloodshot eyes widened in amazement. Before his coding binge, the line-of-sight calculations had used real numbers like 29.4 and 77.258. Real numbers ate up more CPU time since numbers with decimal points had to be more precise. In his stupor, he had replaced all real numbers with integers, which chopped off decimals. The resultant calculations rounded results—less accurate, but close enough, and far more efficient.

"I ran the program, and it ran beautifully, and I looked at the code, and it was some of the prettiest code I'd ever written," Koeneke recalled, laughing.

The fact that Debra Jean embraced rather than tolerated her fiancé's decision to treat the computer lab as a second home proved to Koeneke that she was a keeper. He rarely went home. Every day, he worked on class assignments until five or six. Then he put schoolwork away and brought up *Moria*. A little later, Debra Jean brought dinner. They would catch up on the day's events, and he would go back to coding while she played the latest builds, or prototypes, of the game. Around one or two in the morning, he begrudgingly went home to rest up for work.

> I would do this day in and day out. On the weekends, it was not uncommon for me to work on the game for 12 to 14 hours a day. She'd find a bug and I'd go fix it. It was kind of fun. If we decided we wanted to go out, we'd go out. Go to a movie or whatever, come back and code some more.

> *Right across the floor, close to the feet of two huge pillars, a great fissure had opened. Out of it a fierce red light came, and now and again, flames licked at the brink and curled about the bases of the columns. Wisps of dark smoke wavered in the hot air.*[8]

By the end of the summer, Koeneke had completed *Moria* 1.0. But he was not finished. As he watched Debra Jean and other players go through the dungeons, he began to wonder why he had included gold along with magical weapons and treasures. Gold, a holdover from *Rogue*, was pointless if there was nothing to spend it on.

> I don't know why I thought of this, but somehow I got the idea that the top level should be a town. I came from role-playing games, and in every role-playing game I've played, you come out of dungeons and you can sell all your loot, buy new loot, and go back in.

Where *Rogue* always started players in the first level of the dungeon, *Moria* 2.0 dropped them in a town. Buildings were gray, vaguely blocked-shaped text characters. At the bottom of each was a blank space representing a doorway, and standing in the doorway was a number. The number was a shopkeeper that bought and sold different items. "Town originally required players to barter for every single sell. They hated this. I [revised the code so that] once a price was haggled, it was remembered for future sales."

By the time *Moria* 2.0 emerged, OU's computer labs were crawling with people who wanted to play. Koeneke began immortalizing the exploits of players who survived longer than their peers by creating monsters that bore famous players' names, weapons, and stats. A friend of his, Jimmy Todd, helped him carry the idea of unique characters even further. Todd was a fellow computer science major who, like Koeneke, was bored by the regular curriculum. He wanted something more challenging, and *Moria* fit the bill. He wrote a character generator that let players choose their character's race and class, such as elf archer or human fighter, deepening the player's attachment to his character and adding new layers of strategy such as abilities unique to certain races.

As the codebase evolved, monsters became more fearsome. In the earliest versions of *Moria*, monsters had all behaved the same: when players drew near, monsters moved toward them.

That approach made monsters feel generic, and put a lot of overhead on the VAX computer, which had to calculate monster positions and movements for every player.

In version 2.0, monsters grew even more cunning. "It was all probability driven. Certain creatures had higher or lower probabilities of moving randomly, or moving straight, or casting a spell, or doing things." While browsing the computer's directory of files late one night, he stumbled upon proof that his attempts to imbue denizens with personalities was working better than intended. Manuals had been written by students describing the vindictiveness of this or that monster, and how the monster seemed to remember that players had attacked it earlier. When he approached the authors of the manuals to explain that probabilities and random numbers were pulling the strings, the students politely but firmly silenced him, insisting that they *knew* the monsters were truly sentient.

Koeneke's next move was to diversify the bestiary. Seeing no reason why monsters should be constrained to 26 capital letters, he decided that lowercase letters, uppercase letters, and special text symbols would denote species. For instance, a lowercase "h" stood for human, the base species. Using data structures, he was able to derive subtypes: an "h" could stand for a human mage, a human warrior, or even a human drunkard who stumbled around town picking fights. From there, he color-coded monsters as a way to diversify enemies even further, and to inform observant players. A red letter meant a creature able to deal fire damage, while green monsters spat acid that ate through steel.

No amount of information would ever be enough to make players superior to the foes haunting the mines. Koeneke knew from playing *D&D* that dungeon masters frowned on idleness, so he wrote code that generated new monsters according to a timer. As the timer ticked down, a new monster would appear far from the player's location so the player could not see it pop into existence—meaning no level could ever be completely cleared out.

Monster appearances were mostly random. In one session, players might encounter a particular species of monster. Upon starting a new adventure, that monster may never appear. Only one monster, the Balrog, was guaranteed to challenge players, provided they survived the descent into its lair.

With every update to *Moria*, Koeneke pared his code, wiping out unwieldy commands. For the next major version, 3.0, Koeneke put the algorithms that generated dungeon levels under the knife, writing routines to dig elaborate tunnels, corridors, and rooms. New characters received a pack of gold and basic supplies to give them a leg up, and equipment could be sold for gold, which players could use to purchase better items.

To Koeneke's amazement, demand for *Moria* spread beyond University of Oklahoma. "I got requests to send a tape with my game on it to people all over the world, and one request came from University of Texas. Back then, I was not releasing source code. I just released the executable. So I compiled them a special version," he remembered, chuckling. The Oklahoma Sooners, the football team hailing from Koeneke's alma matter, had been embroiled in a decades-long rivalry with UT's Texas Longhorns. In the version of *Moria* tailor-made for UT, Koeneke created a human monster on the town level called "OU Fan" and gave it the ability to reproduce rapidly and in mass quantities. Then he disabled the game's turn-based mechanism, allowing monsters to move in real-time.

When players from UT extracted the game from the eight-inch tape reel (the standard distribution method for the time), they received a shock. The single OU Fan in town multiplied, becoming two, then four, then sixteen, and onward until the screen teemed with OU Fans that converged on the helpless "@" avatar. "I got a note back from University of Texas that read, 'Ha ha, very funny. Can we have the real game now?' I just changed a few bytes in the executable to turn it off. I guess they didn't see the humor in it that I did."

> *It came to the edge of the fire and the light faded as if a cloud had bent over it. Then with a rush it leaped across the fissure. The flames roared up to greet it, and wreathed about it; and a black smoke swirled in the air. Its streaming mane kindled, and blazed behind it. In its right hand was a blade like a stabbing tongue of fire; in its left it held a whip of many thongs.*[9]

Written near the end of 1985, *Moria* 4.0 gave way to even more improvements. While the vast majority of the mines were generated according to algorithms and random numbers, Koeneke introduced special rooms that followed pre-constructed templates. These rooms held some of the greatest treasures players could find in the mines, and were guarded by elite monsters. Still looking for ways to give new players a leg up, Koeneke added a new ability called mining. Armed with the right equipment, players could dig ore from walls and sell it for gold.

All the while, the Balrog, Durin's Bane, ran roughshod over adventurers.

> He's a tenacious fighter. He would do smart things that other creatures wouldn't do, like teleport you to him. He could get really nasty. But the other thing he could do is if he got hurt, he would try to run away and heal. Then you'd have to hunt him down, and by then he got more of his hit points back. So if you killed a Balrog, you got a feeling of accomplishment.

One afternoon, a friend of Koeneke's named William Ouchark let out a triumphant yell. Ouchark had toppled Durin's Bane—or so it seemed. "I was stunned," Koeneke said. "What I did was I sat down and interviewed him so I could find out how he beat it. I wanted to make certain that he didn't do it through a defect in the game."

As it turned out, Ouchark had exploited a hole in the Balrog's logic. Stepping into a new dungeon, he had cleared out a few rooms until he rounded a corner and spotted the dreaded "B" at the far end of the hall. The Balrog teleported Ouchark to him and dug in, dealing tremendous damage with his whip and fiery breath. But Ouchark was tenacious. The combatants went toe to toe until the Balrog abruptly withdrew, limping around a corner where it could heal. Ouchark rushed after it—then, struck by sudden inspiration, he ducked into a nearby room and placed himself on the opposite side of the wall where the Balrog hunkered. He realized that he could cast fireballs *through the wall*, dealing residual damage to the Balrog. A few fireballs later, Durin's Bane was no more.

Far from being annoyed, Koeneke admired Ouchark's ingenuity. He paid tribute to his friend's victory in a unique way. Ouchark had played a gnome named Iggy, so Koeneke created a gnome monster called "The Evil Iggy." Ouchark's doppelganger marked the first player to be immortalized as a monster in *Moria*. "I also made it so that damage would not penetrate the walls, so future players had to find other ways to kill the beast."

In the spring of 1986, Koeneke, nearing the end of his time in school, put the finishing touches on *Moria* 4.5. Uncertain of what would become of his game after he left, he made the decision to release it to the public.

I never would have written that game if I hadn't run into *Colossal Cave* and *Rogue*, and those were free. What I did is I ended up releasing the source code to anyone who wanted to run the game, but also so people could learn the same things I had learned—about data structures, about how to write code efficiently. That was kind of my gift to the education world, I guess.

After graduating, Koeneke got a job at American Airlines as a programmer. He soon got caught up in the fascinating challenges of his job and left *Moria* in the hands of students at University of Oklahoma who had expressed interest in maintaining the game. He kept track of their progress for about a year, calling occasionally to find out how things were going. Eventually, his schedule swept all thoughts of *Moria* from his mind.

In 1993, Koeneke discovered a technological marvel called the Internet. Two years later, he ran a search for *Moria* out of idle curiosity. To his astonishment, he turned up page after page of *Moria* message boards and clones modeled after his work. Touched and pleased that *Moria* had survived the jump to the online age, he joined one of the message boards and wrote a post asking if one game in particular was related in any way to his contribution to what had become known as roguelike role-playing games. When he next opened his inbox, he was flooded with emails from excited gamers who were either ecstatic or skeptical over his claim that he was the creator of *Moria*.

Some of Koeneke's game-design heroes had even taken notice. "*Moria* is probably the closest to what I wanted to do when I made *Rogue*," Michael Toy admitted during our interviews. "It's got shops, and all the monsters are really different. When I played *Moria*, I felt like, yeah, this is what I wanted to get *Rogue* to do."

Koeneke read through some of the emails, then turned his attention back to two *Moria* clones that had captured his attention. One was *UMoria*, an adaptation written by James E. "Jim" Wilson of UC Berkeley. Wilson's goal had been to port Koeneke's game over to a multitude of other computer platforms so that more players could enjoy it, as well as add more features and squash a few bugs in Koeneke's code.[10]

The other, the game he correctly presumed was a spiritual successor to his, was named after another location in Tolkien's *Lord of the Rings* universe—a location that inspired even greater dread in players than the Mines of Moria.

Far beneath the ruined halls of Angband, Balrogs lurked still, forever awaiting the return of their Lord. And he being freed gathered again all his servants that he could find, and came to the ruins of Angband. There he delved anew his vast vaults and dungeons, and above their gates he reared the threefold peaks of Thangorodrim, and a great reek of dark smoke was ever wreathed about them.[11]

* * *

Side Quests

(Turn to page 83 for Chapter 8)

Koeneke's Early Games

Determined to create a more freeform game, Koeneke got hold of a TI-59 calculator around 1978 and put it through its paces by writing *Maze*, a dungeon game. The game code was stored on a magnetic card that users slotted into the calculator. At the outset, *Maze* put together a randomly generated maze consisting of 20 rooms. Each room had four exits, and a handful of monsters patrolled the maze arbitrarily. As a bonus feature, players could connect the TI-59 calculator running the game to a thermal printer and study their route as they traversed the dungeon.

> There were several named treasure rooms like the Emerald Room you had to find to win. As you moved from room to room you got a reading of doorways; *Emerald Room: N__W* [meant] a door to the north and a door to the west. When you met up with a named monster, you could fight or retreat.[12]

The Sphinx was a larger version of *Pyramid* that ate up the entire 48K of memory available on TRS-80 Model I computers, featured a smarter noun-verb interpreter able to digest compound sentences, and saved the player's progress on a cassette tape so they could pick up where they left off. *Daniel's Manor* was even more ambitious. Koeneke realized that very few students on campus had been able to enjoy *The Sphinx* because only a small percentage of them owned TRS-80 Model I's with the necessary 48K of memory. *Daniel's Manor*, which took place in a haunted house, was composed of three distinct modules, each of which ran in 16K of memory. Each module featured a different area replete with its own puzzles, such as the haunted woods outside the mansion. Most interestingly, players could rewrite the modules to contain unique areas and puzzles, effectively enabling anyone who had the game to transform it into their own adventure. Koeneke received loads of requests for the game and put it up on a bulletin board service (BBS) so anyone could play.

Through the Curtain

Koeneke's most baffling and legally questionable request for *Moria* came from Romania, Hungary, and other countries from behind the Iron Curtain. At the time, the U.S. government imposed strict import/export laws that banned computer hardware and software, among other items, from entering areas locked away behind the Curtain.

> The Soviet Union was illegally importing the advanced VAX computers any way they could find. The United States banned the export of the VAX computer chip, because it was so advanced, to the Soviet Union and any of its allies, including China.

Amused that gamers were willing to risk severe penalties just to play *Moria*, yet intimidated by the legal hammer that would drop on him for answering them in the affirmative, Koeneke played the part of law-abiding citizen.

I would go ahead and send them the tape, because they already had a machine, but I pinned a letter on it saying, 'Sorry, I can't send you anything. The FBI might be watching.' But I made sure it was included. I just didn't want to get on an FBI watch list.

The Lost Moria *5.0*

Koeneke did not see *Moria* 4.5 as an end to the adventures in the mines. Before leaving university, he coded a litany of features to include in 5.0, the version he believed would come the closest to realizing the grand vision he'd had for his *Rogue* clone since deciding to build on the foundation Toy, Wichman, and Ken Arnold had lain.

Players could throw flasks of oil that ignited like fireballs upon impact, wear crowns and carry scepters that bestowed new powers, and hire humanoids and animal creatures like human priests who would battle (and heal) alongside players over a single level. Water was added, which allowed the procedural-generation algorithms to insert streams, flooded rooms, and even aquatic levels.

Curvaceous nymphs and dryads, another type of mercenary, stood a chance of falling in love with players, and would follow them from level to level until they or the player fell in battle. If players had taken care of their companion during the quest, companions could resurrect fallen player-characters—provided they had gathered enough power. Power was accumulated over time; the longer a companion journeyed with the player, the more power they arrogated. Performing a resurrection reset the companion's power to zero, restarting the whole process.

Notes

1. I have heard that there are still forgotten treasures: Tolkien, J.R.R. *The Lord of the Rings Part One: The Fellowship of the Ring*. New York: Ballantine Books.
2. I investigated, and found a small crowd of students: Email message to author, June 12th, 2012. (Author's note: Robert Koeneke explained that he wrote down as many memories of the development of *Moria* as he could dig up and posted them on his now-defunct website, koeneke.com. He was kind enough to send the archived materials to me, which proved a helpful supplement to our interviews and my research.)
3. Ibid.
4. I guess what fascinated me about *Rogue*: Interview with Robert Koeneke. Unless cited otherwise, quotes from Mr. Koeneke come from our interviews conducted over 2012.
5. All about them as they lay hung the darkness: Tolkien, J.R.R. *The Lord of the Rings Part One: The Fellowship of the Ring*. New York: Ballantine Books.
6. Ibid.
7. Breaking ground in 1981: Email message to author, June 12, 2012. (Author's note: All dates pertaining to the release of new versions of *Moria* come from documents sent to me by Robert Koeneke.)
8. Right across the floor, close to the feet: Tolkien, J.R.R. *The Lord of the Rings Part One: The Fellowship of the Ring*. New York: Ballantine Books.
9. Ibid.
10. Wilson's goal had been to port Koeneke's game: "*Moria* vs. *UMoria*." *Google Groups*. https://groups.google.com/forum/#!topic/rec.games.moria/TIt1PhDLz8s.
11. Far beneath the ruined halls of Angband: Tolkien, J.R.R. *The Silmarillion*. New York: Random House.
12. There were several named treasure rooms: Email message to author, June 12, 2012. (Author's note: This reference can be found in the Side Quest supplementary material for this chapter.)

8

Neapolitan Roguelike
The Many Flavors of Angband

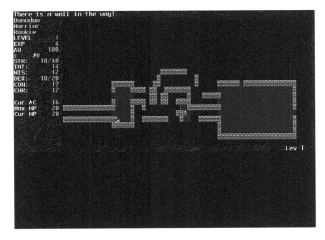

Many versions of *Angband*, such as the MS-DOS port shown above, offer graphical interfaces. (Image: Mobygames.)

Arcane Games

Andi Sidwell was not sure what to make of the information displayed on the computer their big brothers shared. Antony was 20, and Peter was 24. The brothers, who had gone in together on a house, were always introducing 10-year-old Andi to hobbies and ideas. This one, a computer game called *Moria*, left them bewildered … and intrigued.

Sidwell leaned in closer to the monitor. *Moria* was a game, yet there were no colorful graphics. Text characters formed the corridors and chambers of a vast dungeon. There were other symbols strewn around the screen: colorful letters that their brothers said represented fearsome monsters, as well as characters that stood for traps and treasure.

Sidwell was no stranger to esoteric computer programs. At the age of eight, they had come across a programming textbook for the BBC BASIC language used to write software on the BBC Micro, a PC manufactured by Acorn Computers. Later that year, older brother Antony had come home for a visit and brought his work with him; he was writing an application in a language called C. One afternoon, he got up and left the computer. Sidwell crept over to take a look. Antony's compiler, the program in which C programmers wrote and tested code, filled the screen. Slipping into the chair, Sidwell studied the syntax for a few moments, then began to tinker. "It was pretty unusual for someone my age to be doing that. It seems like that experience is more typical for people five to 10 years older than me—but even then, I suppose, still only for the geekiest part of the population."[1]

Moria stumped Sidwell. Determined to understand the game, Sidwell borrowed a copy of *Moria* from Peter and Antony. Weeks later, Sidwell had made little progress. The arrow keys moved the character, a little "@" symbol, but the deluge of other in-game actions left them stymied. Every key on the keyboard made something happen, and there were so many commands to remember. Something different happened depending on whether Sidwell pressed a lowercase "d" or an uppercase "D." Frustrated, they gave up.

In 1997, the Sidwell family connected their RiscPC—a successor to the BBC Micro—to the Internet. Once online, Sidwell's world shrank, but in the best possible way. With a click, Sidwell could visit the online homes of people who lived on the other sides of oceans—and download games for free. "I downloaded them systematically, tried the ones I liked, and junked the ones I didn't. There was a lot of crap."

Moria, it seemed, was not crap. People online seemed to love it, but for Sidwell, the game remained inscrutable. Sidwell had even tried *UMoria*, but it, too, proved confusing and frustrating. While on the hunt for new games to try, Sidwell came across a dungeon hack that had been baked in a similar mold. "At some point I must have come across *Angband*, and it was like an easier to use version of *UMoria*."

Angband was easier to play, though it was not the most entertaining game. Like *Moria*, all the action took place in dungeons. Sidwell did some digging and found that *Angband* was like ice cream: there were many flavors, and they had sampled vanilla first. The other flavors were called variants, derivatives of vanilla *Angband* that featured different settings, monsters, and magical items. "Soon after, I discovered *Zangband* […] in 1999. I loved that game and played it loads. I was curious so I downloaded the source code and read it."

Fueled by curiosity, Sidwell began to code.

"You Have a Superb Feeling…"

With each cassette tape containing *Moria* that creator Robert Koeneke had mailed out, the virtual mines grew, ensnaring players around the world eager for a taste of randomly generated treasure. James Wilson, a student at University of California Berkeley, got addicted to the game and decided to port it to *UNIX*. He called it *UMoria*, and released the first version in 1989. A year later, Alex Cutler and Andy Astrand, students attending University of Warwick, played the game and harbored the same ambitions toward *UMoria* that Koeneke had harbored toward *Rogue* seven years previous. They wanted more. More items, more monsters—more everything.

Moria lasted 50 levels, the last of which contained the dreaded Balrog. Cutler and Astrand doubled the count. The new master of the dungeon was Morgoth, known in Tolkien lore as the Black Foe of the World. Cutler and Astrand kept the Balrog, but demoted it. One Balrog made the bravest heroes quake in their boots, but the Black Foe had spawned legions of Balrogs to serve him. Even Sauron, the primary antagonist in J.R.R. Tolkien's *The Lord of the Rings* novels, was merely a lieutenant under Morgoth.

Tolkien's writings loosely guided Cutler and Astrand's design. To change things up, they scrapped the Mines of Moria and changed the setting to Angband, a fortress built by Morgoth beneath a mountain chain. Trolls, dragons, Ringwraiths, and other horrors from Tolkien's stories haunted Angband's halls, and were joined by unique monsters, powerful foes bearing the names and abilities of Morgoth's most powerful servants. Durin's Bane, the Balrog from *Moria*, was one. Sauron was another.

Players began their adventure through *Angband* by choosing from dozens of races and classes, then materialized in the town level, which reflected the settlement in *Moria*. A staircase near one of the shops led down to the first level of the dungeon. To heighten the sense of foreboding as players fought their way down, Cutler and Astrand marked their progress by depth instead of levels, as Robert Koeneke had done in *Moria*. Every level was 50 feet deeper than the last, which meant players had to descend through 5,000 feet of tricks, traps, and battles to stand a chance of confronting Morgoth, a gray "P" that had the power to smash through walls and summon dragons to his aid.

Upon graduating, Cutler and Astrand left *Angband* behind and moved on to other interests. Sean Marsh and Geoff Hill, two students who had pitched in on *Angband*'s development, had no desire to see the game wither. They spent months adding artifacts and tightening algorithms. As Warwick students fought their way deeper into the game, Marsh and Hill generated a list of the most accomplished questers and posted it to the rec.games.moria newsgroup. Across the newsgroup and popular hacker channels, whispers of a public release of the game spread. That was exactly what Marsh and Hill had wanted. They had made the list of winners public in order to generate buzz: a successor to *Moria*, bigger, better, and tougher, was coming.[2]

On April 11th, 1993, Marsh and Hill released *Angband* version "2.4.frog-knows" (2.4.fk) for *UNIX*, marking the first time the game had set foot outside University of Warwick. The public release included dozens of character races and classes, special rooms known as vaults where powerful foes guarded the best magical artifacts, and level feelings—printed messages intended to convey the level of danger and quality of items at the current depth. When players entered a new dungeon, the game analyzed the level and calculated a rating based on the monsters, vaults, and artifacts within. The higher the rating, the better the level feeling, which ranged from *What a boring place…* all the way up to *You have a superb feeling about this level*.

But *Angband* was not finished yet.

The Years of the Lamps

Unbeknownst to them, Marsh and Hill had started a chain reaction. Shortly after they made *Angband* public, another programmer named Charles Teague pulled 2.4.fk from the newsgroup and converted it to MS-DOS so PC gamers could meet their fate in Morgoth's fortress. Teague continued to update the game until March 1994 when he rolled out *Angband* v1.4 and disappeared from the newsgroup, likely because real-life obligations grew too overwhelming.[3]

Concurrently to Teague's work on the PC adaptation, Charles Swiger began to examine the game's workings. His goal was to clean up the code and filter suggestions from players on the newsgroup, as well as authors of *Angband* flavors, variants to the game's source code. One of the most popular features of PC *Angband* 1.4 was colorized text, used by authors to distinguish monsters. For example, the Balrog of Moria appeared as a violet "U." Swiger, *Angband's* self-appointed maintainer, rolled the change and other suitable modifications into the next version of the game. Years later, official releases of *Angband* would be known as "vanilla *Angband*," the codebase and starting point from which any developer was welcome to develop other flavors for free distribution.

In late 1994, Swiger dropped a bombshell on the *Angband* faithful. He had found a job and no longer had time to maintain the vanilla game's code. Like the Tolkien world from which the game drew inspiration, factions arose and nominated contenders to vie for the position of god of the code. They knew that to be the maintainer of vanilla *Angband* was to become as powerful as Tolkien's Eru Ilúvatar, divine creator of the world. Each contender argued his or her merits, yet arguing was all that filled the empty void. The throne lay vacant.

On New Year's Day 1995, Ben Harrison made the decision for them.[4] He had been playing the Apple Macintosh version of the game when a debilitating bug crippled his progress. Occasionally, an *M* would appear on-screen, signaling the appearance of a manticore—a monster with the body of a lion, the head of a human, and a mouth full of fangs. The manticore attacked by spitting fangs, and triggered the message *The manticore shoots spikes -more-*, signaling that the player should press the spacebar to advance the fight. But because of the bug, the message repeated endlessly, forcing players to abort the game and lose their progress.

"The thrill. The immersion. The randomness of the levels. The excitement of realizing that you had found a magic item, or better yet, an artifact. The heart wrenching despair of falling through a trap door while running towards the glowing yellow tilde [representing a magical phial] in the corner of the room, and realizing that you had missed your one and only chance— back then—of acquiring the Phial of Galadriel," waxed Harrison, recalling the thrill of adventure and the close shaves he had survived (or not) that had given rise to his *Angband* addiction. "Some of my fondest memories involve drinking a random potion with bated breath, knowing it might be deadly, but unable to resist the lure of knowledge."[5]

While the rest of the *Angband* newsgroup community squabbled, Harrison quietly set about patching and organizing the game's cluttered code. His updates were like corks that plugged the holes left by Swiger's sudden departure. Unaware that so much debate had raged around the maintainership, Harrison was surprised when the code he had submitted on January 1 was declared the official 2.7.0 version, and that he, Harrison, had been appointed the new maintainer by proxy.

Harrison's efforts to organize *Angband's* underpinnings resulted in code that was easy to read and edit. Retroactively, *Angband* maintainers refer to his work as the great code clean-up. "Keep it clean, make it elegant," Harrison told me, summarizing his goals during his time as maintainer.

The great code clean-up benefitted other developers, too. Easier-to-read code allowed more programmers than ever to try their hand at downloading the source files and writing modules that added mechanics, artifacts, monsters, and spells, as well as spin off their own flavors of *Angband* that featured unique themes and settings. Other programmers concentrated on porting the game to a wider range of operating systems including Windows, Linux, and permutations of IBM workstations. Modules written by developers on the newsgroup often found their way into the vanilla codebase, provided the maintainer deemed the changes they introduced appropriate or exemplary.

"Actually, I [cleaned up the codebase] to simplify compilation on the Mac, for which large static code files were difficult to compile," Harrison admitted. "The customization benefit was actually an unintentional side effect."

For five years, each subsequent update from Harrison optimized *Angband* further, as well as folded in prime suggestions from the game's growing legion of fans. Like Smaug's horde of treasures, the game's trove of artifacts grew more and more resplendent while the monsters set to guard them grew greater in number and strength.

By the time he released 2.8.3, Harrison had succumbed to real-life responsibilities. Robert Rühlmann was next in the line of succession.

The Years of the Trees

In 2000, Rühlmann—known by the handle rr9 on the newsgroup—released an unofficial update. His version was a hodgepodge of bug fixes and features submitted by other players: the easy patch, an update created by Tim Baker that simplified the process of springing traps and opening doors; advanced artificial intelligence for monsters written by Keldon Jones; and randomized properties on artifacts, an enhancement created by Greg Wooledge. As Harrison had done, the simple act of taking charge was enough to anoint Rühlmann the keeper of the code. A few years of patches and updates followed until, inevitably, he announced that other obligations would force him to abdicate the throne.

Once again, diehard supporters who had been writing their own flavors or submitting fixes to the vanilla codebase threw their names into the hat. Among them was Andi Sidwell, known among other *Angband* players by the online handle takkaria. "The big change happened when rr9 [Rühlmann] said he didn't have time to continue," Sidwell recalled.

> Unusually, he actually wrote to the newsgroup saying that he was going to stop working on the game and announced the search for a successor. There was a lot of private discussion amongst people who wanted to make their case for taking over.

Competition was fierce. Leon Marrick, one of the frontrunners, was the creator of *Oangband*, a flavor renowned for superb item and monster balance; and *Sangband*, short for *Skills Angband*, one of the oldest flavors as well as one of the first to introduce unique character skills such as crafting armor, greater proficiency with certain types of weapons, and modes of unarmed combat such as wrestling and karate.[6] Another candidate, Bahman Rabii, was Marrick's successor on *Oangband*. Timo Pietilä was a long-time player who had an eye for refining gameplay.

Rühlmann may or may not have been aware that there was any discussion around who would take his place; in March 2006, he unwittingly ended the debate by selecting Julian Lighton—perhaps, Sidwell posited, due to Lighton's conservatism toward the game, which appealed to long-time players. Lighton proved a divisive choice. He pushed out a few updates and then went quiet in 2007. Discontent rumbled up from the community. Sensing that Lighton might be stepping away from maintainership, Sidwell took stock of features players wanted to see.

> I had been producing patches for some time, a lot of them just importing the interface features I missed from variants into *Angband* proper. Vanilla is something like the tree of life for variants, or at least was once upon a time, and I thought that improving vanilla would mean that future variants would have a better base to build on.

In an announcement email made to variant authors and players, Sidwell made it clear that they were not attempting to usurp Lighton's position as maintainer; their patches were merely an attempt to prevent *Angband* from rusting. Sidwell's changes were embraced by the community.

However, Sidwell was not looking to take over. They merely hoped that pushing out updates would light a fire under Lighton to return to work. Another variant author, Nick McConnell, paid a visit to the *Angband* newsgroup and lit a fire of his own.

> **From: Nick McConnell**
> **Subject: Angband maintainer**
> **Date: 2007-03-23 13:19:35**
> **OK, someone needs to say it.**
> **Andrew Sidwell should be the Angband maintainer.**
> **Comments from anyone, particularly Julian [Lighton], encouraged.**
> **Nick.**[6]

Sidwell discovered the thread and was amazed to see a string of replies echoing McConnell's sentiment. Pleased, Sidwell wasted little time getting to work.

> I remember when I was first taking over, I was mostly interested in implementing what you might call the consensus position. I made exhaustive lists of ideas and suggestions that others mentioned on the newsgroup; I had several different text files and over a period of months, read many arguments and copied and pasted into my text files some things I liked, and some I didn't. I came to a decent understanding of some issues this way, and eventually condensed my text files down into bullet points for implementation.

Sifting through topic after topic on the game's official forums, Sidwell paid special attention to arguments that broke out over polarizing features. One debate revolved around item degradation and how players used gold. Items degraded as players attacked and took damage, causing them to pour all their gold into costly repairs, which was not as fun or interesting as saving up to buy new items. After weighing community feedback, Sidwell introduced repair-item scrolls that restored items to good-as-new status. When people complained that the scrolls were overpowered—presumably because they allowed players to cling to tried-and-true items rather than branch out and try new ones—Sidwell removed the scrolls.

"The arguments that happened on the newsgroup, and later on the forums, really shaped my view of what my maintainership should be about—which really was following the lead of the community, neither going too slow or too fast, and trying to bring people along with each advancement," Sidwell explained.

Angband's community responded well to Sidwell's transparency. Previous maintainers had been wizards behind curtains, shaping the game in the way they thought would be best. Sidwell emerged from behind the curtain to take stock of what the players wanted while also incorporating the cream of the crop from the many flavors floating around online.

After a year or two, Sidwell took the next logical step and converted *Angband*'s monarchy into a meritocracy. Chris Carr, who had taken an interest in submitting ideas for fixes and features after Harrison's great code clean-up, was one of the first to join.

> [Sidwell] said, 'I'm not going to do the dictatorial maintainer-type thing where people send me patches and I'll decide whether or not to include it, and control everything, and release the game as and when I feel like it. I'm going to create a development team.'[7]

Carr had been a member of *Angband*'s community for years, migrating from the newsgroup to the forums. He had added his voice to Nick McConnell's when McConnell had proposed that Andi Sidwell assume the throne.

Carr had already been in an active role in *Angband*'s development.

> I had submitted patches to previous maintainers to fix and improve the random-artifact generator, but they had never actually been incorporated [into the official version]. Around 2009, I got in touch with takkaria [Sidwell] and said, 'I'd be really interested in joining your devteam. Here's my first contribution; tell me what you think.' I was made to feel very welcome. My patch was incorporated pretty much straightaway, and I received lots of testing and feedback.

Around the time Carr expressed interest in joining the DevTeam, several others were welcomed into the fold. Like Sidwell, Erik Osheim was at first bemused and then entranced by the cryptic nature of roguelike games. While in college in 2004, Osheim downloaded an update to the game that added a chart that listed the name of every monster and the colored letter that represented it—*Baby Green Dragon* and a green lowercase *d*, for example. Being able to reference the chart when a monster appeared enabled Osheim to recognize beasts that had given him trouble in the past, and determine whether it would be best to confront or sneak past them.

He found the monster chart so helpful that he decided to create a chart for items. "Items are the same way: you see a brown comma or gray slash, but you don't know what it is. I wanted [an item chart] to exist, but it didn't. So I said, 'I know how to code C. I could probably figure this out.'"[8] After downloading the code and learning how everything fit together, he submitted his patch and kept his fingers crossed that Sidwell would merge it into the main game. "I earned the trust of Andi Sidwell and became part of the devteam. I picked up bugs from the bug tracker and started fixing them, and becoming familiar with the codebase."

Aaron Bader was another who earned Sidwell's respect by taking initiative.

> I was posting on the forums a lot, and I think I made a comment like, 'Yeah, I'd like to modify the code, but I'm not sure how to get started.' They said, 'Just come on the dev channel. We'll help you get set up.' I guess a lot of people are bluffing: 'Oh, yeah, I would totally help, but it's too hard to get started.' But I took them up on that offer, and they helped me get set up. I started playing around with the code.[9]

Simulating Virtual Reality

To encourage more community members to get involved in development, Sidwell moved vanilla *Angband*'s code to Github (pronounced "get-hub"), a repository where any number of people can submit changes to code. Previously, *Angband* had been stored on Subversion (SVN), a repository that made it difficult to keep track of which sections of code had been changed. Users who modified the same section often received errors if their changes did not jive with modifications another user had submitted before them. Github merged code automatically, facilitating organization.

Meanwhile, the DevTeam tightened loose screws. To expunge tedium and keep the game challenging yet fair, they focused on balancing procedurally generated elements. A physicist by day, Aaron Bader enjoyed writing simulations to solve problems at work and in *Angband*. Years of playing the game had left him with burning questions, such as how often certain monsters tended to spawn and whether or not particular items dropped too often.

> When you're playing, you really have such a small sample size. But with statistics-gathering, you get actual data. Like, okay, this is a 1-in-1,000 event; this is a 1-in-100 event; this is a 1-in-10 event. You can really answer some of the questions that are impossible to answer from the player's standpoint.

Searching for a reliable method able to produce definitive answers, Bader employed the Monte Carlo method. Often used to solve complex physics problems, the Monte Carlo method applies a series of algorithms that obtain numerical information from repeated samplings of randomized data. *Angband* is programmed to only generate certain monsters and items once the player reaches certain depths. By feeding his Monte Carlo algorithms data such as which monsters and items are allowed to generate, Bader can observe how often they appear on certain levels.

> For me, the aspect that's interesting is the game never plays the same way. Your capabilities are always different. Every once in a while, you'll use items you've never used before, just because it happens that they're the best items you have in that particular play-through.

Likewise, Erik Osheim runs simulations for the purpose of studying which monsters are able to appear at certain depths. Out-of-depth monsters, those that would normally appear on deeper, tougher levels, are allowed to pop up earlier so long as their presence does not become cloying.

> We want [randomized experiences] within parameters. Either there should be no chance of an encounter with, say, a great wyrm [dragon] on level 1 at all, or [the odds] should be so low that they're basically zero. Most players will never see it. And those [odds] basically end up being the same thing. If a person dies to a super-powerful enemy once, they might complain, but as long as it doesn't happen a lot, it's not really a big deal.

Running simulations is critical to maintaining balance in *Angband*. Unlike *NetHack* and *Rogue*, *Angband* generates new dungeons when players return to levels they cleared. Players tend to fall into two camps. Those who like to clear the same level over and over in the hopes of finding top-tier items known to appear there; and those who prefer to clear a level once and then forge

I think what I would regard as core traditions are the dependence on character progression by items, and the capacity to play at one's own pace. There are also, of course, many monsters and items which are beloved—or deeply hated—and which I would not want to mess with too much. Also: permadeath.

Test of Time

For over 20 years, the titanic doors of Morgoth's fortress have creaked open, swallowing hapless and hearty adventurers alike. Thousands have ventured into the labyrinth, and the DevTeam—McConnell, Bader, Carr, Osheim, and Robert Au—believe thousands more will brave its depths so long as one tradition remains sacrosanct:

> "It's very clear that what has kept *Angband* going is that maintainers have graciously stepped down and handed over the reins. No one has ever said, 'This is my game. I get to decide what it is, and I don't want to work on it anymore, but no one else can either.' Every time a maintainer has stepped down, they've passed the torch amicably to the next person," Bader explained.

Sidwell speculates that interest will continue indefinitely due to cheap, widely available Internet access, which facilitated rapid growth of the game and its community beginning in the 1990s.

> There was an outpouring of innovation when variants started being made and they all provide quite a different gaming experience. In some sense it makes a lot of sense to have so many variants; if everyone tried to work on one game, you would have an unintelligible and broken mess. This way you get cross-pollination of ideas, copying of code, and so on. I think it's probably a good reason why *Angband* has stayed going.

Most importantly, a text-only game that originated on a dumb terminal did not seem outdated—not then, and not now, when the imagination still remains a more powerful graphics processor than the most lavish video card. "Every few years, somebody tries to make a multiplayer version [of *Angband*], or a version with 'better' graphics, but that is, in my opinion, missing the point," Harrison stated.

New players find their way onto the forums, ask questions, and begin their quest. Osheim believes it should be the goal of all DevTeam members to make the descent into darkness as welcoming as possible.

> I think that despite the fact that it's a somewhat challenging game, I think the experience could be much more welcoming for new players. Some games have a tutorial mode. I would love it if Angband had more of that stuff. We have some things like that, but we have a long way to go.

*   *   *

Side Quests

(Turn to page 97 for Chapter 9)

Assimilation

While Harrison kept elegance and organization at the top of his priority list, he made plenty of other changes to the code. He added inscriptions on items that made their abilities clearer, an options menu where players could configure the game more to their liking, a bot—known as the borg—able to play the game of its own accord, and, with the help of a friend and fellow programmer, tighter line-of-sight code engineered to benefit players stuck using older hardware.

> Run through the town and watch the floor light up, and you are seeing the most obvious use of the new code. But it provided a massive efficiency boost which was particularly important on lower-end machines. Programmers these days are spoiled by fast machines.

Deep, Dark Secrets

Establishing a team of maintainers allowed Sidwell to cover up what many might have viewed as a weakness. "The big secret is that I'm a crap player and I'm bad at balancing," Sidwell admitted. "My main attempt at re-balancing the game—around the 3.1 series [of updates]—was, if not a failure, definitely an indication to me that I should try to find other people who had a better sense."

With a team more interested in addressing game balance, Sidwell could stick to streamlining the game's code by building on top of the spring cleaning Harrison had performed, and adding in more variation to present an even more unique experience to players every time they ventured inside Morgoth's fortress.

Farming

For a long time, the majority of players were hanging around levels where potions that increased stats appeared. "When we find tactics we don't love, we'll subtly incentivize it or remove incentives from doing it. We don't want to outright ban it or say it's cheap," Osheim clarified. The DevTeam countered item-grinding tactics by widening the curve on stat-gain potions, making them appear more frequently at lower depths. In recent years, empirical data has confirmed a predilection for deep-diving, moving to the bottom of the dungeon as quickly as possible in order to find better treasure. Most players understand that the trick to deep-diving is to avoid monsters whenever possible.

Transitioning to a team-based approach didn't go off without a hitch. "I happened to join around the same time as a couple of other guys, and the game entered a period of very, very rapid change, which had its pros and cons in the community," Carr recalled.

Feedback

Before the advent of the World Wide Web, Usenet, a discussion board where users could post and reply to notes, was one of the primary methods of communication online. As the Web spun farther and farther, Internet connectivity became cheaper. Communities picked up stakes from Usenet and relocated to websites that made it easier to host files. Over 2009 and 2010, *Angband*'s players went with them.

The move to Github and the Web resulted in an explosion of productivity for the DevTeam. New versions appeared for download almost every night. Realizing that they needed to delineate the vanilla version of the game from experiments that may or may not be integrated into the codebase, the DevTeam created separate branches. There was the main branch, which hosted the latest version that anyone could download, play, and modify. Then there was a development branch, where DevTeam members could conduct experiments like mad scientists. It did not matter if their tinkering broke vital components, since their experiments took place on a separate branch than the main codebase.

Still advocating transparency, Sidwell made the development branch visible to the community. Community members were welcome to download the works-in-progress and comment on the embryonic ideas modeled therein. The forums hosted roughly 300 active users at any given time, and only a fraction of those bothered to climb up to the development branch and sample its fruit. Those who did had a lot to say.

"The people on the forum thought that what was in the development version was the way the game was going," Carr admitted.

> There wasn't a lot of clarity of, 'These are development builds, so stuff can be reversed and re-balanced at any time.' There was a lot of arguing and discontentment about some of the changes. Some of us, including me, spent far too much time and energy arguing on the forum instead of developing the game.

One of the ongoing experiments on the development branch centered on rebalancing ego items, weapons and armor that sported special properties. The DevTeam was trying to determine the rate at which ego items could be generated. At any given time in the trial-and-error code, ego items were as bountiful as tiles of stone on the floor, or as rare as a dragon on level 1. Believing that the code foreshadowed things to come in updates, members of the community ranted and raved about the rate of items drops. The DevTeam's transparency had backfired.

Eventually, the issue was sewn up. The DevTeam created a third branch called *Angband 4*, overtly demarcated from the 3.x series of updates. Community members grew to understand that only code on the 3.x branch would be found in official releases, while *Angband 4* was more like a secret lab where the Dr. Frankensteins of the DevTeam created and killed features on a whim.

Gradually, outcry on the forums died down. Rather than members of the DevTeam needing to shout over everyone, community members who had been around to see the experiments explode in everyone's faces were able to explain how the branches worked to newcomers. For anyone still grumbling over changes in any branch, there was always an easy fix available: download the code and create a variant.

Notes

1. It was pretty unusual for someone my age: Interview with Andi Sidwell. All quotes from Andi Sidwell come from interviews conducted via email over 2014.
2. Indeed, *Angband*'s curators: "Angband Releases: 2.4.frog-knows." *@ngband*. http://rephial.org/release/2.4.fk.

3. Teague continued to update the game: "Angband Releases: PCAngband 1.4." *@ngband*. http://rephial.org/release/pcangband-1.4.

4. On New Year's Day 1995: "Version Information." *@ngband*. http://rephial.org/help/version. (Author's note: From this point on in the chapter, I refrained from citing dates on which updates to *Angband* were released, since they can easily be found on the *Angband* development page, cited here.)

5. The thrill: Interview with Ben Harrison. All quotes from Ben Harrison come from interviews conducted over 2014.

6. From: Nick McConnell: " rec.games.roguelike.angband looking glass." *Angband.oook.cz*. http://angband.oook.cz/rgra.php?showpost=93590.

7. Chris Carr, who had taken an interest: Interview with Chris Carr. All quotes from Andi Sidwell come from interviews conducted over 2014.

8. Items are the same way: Interview with Erik Osheim. All quotes from Erik Osheim come from interviews conducted over 2014.

9. Aaron Bader was one who earned Sidwell's respect: Interview with Aaron Bader. All quotes from Aaron Bader come from interviews conducted over 2014.

10. October 22, 2013: "New vision for Angband—Part 1." *Angband.oook.cz*. http://angband.oook.cz/forum/showthread.php?t=6371&page=5.

11. I'm a big Tolkien fan: Interview with Nick McConnell. All quotes from Nick McConnell come from interviews conducted over 2014.

9

Wish You Were Here!
Questing for Postcards in Ancient Domains of Mystery

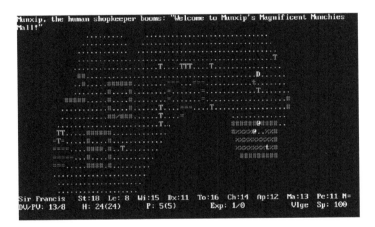

ADOM's overworld includes plains, trees, rivers, and (of course) dungeons. (Image: Mobygames.)

Decisions

Sitting back from the table, Thomas Biskup swept his eyes over its contents. Pencils, many worn down to the nub. Multi-sided dice, each a different color. Notebook paper covered in scribbles. Maps depicting half-finished land masses. Four guidebooks to pen-and-paper role-playing games in various stages of completion. Behind him, a computer hummed. The screen was dark; the screensaver timer had expired, putting the monitor into a rest state. Biskup envied it.

He had a decision to make.

Biskup was in Thailand, vacationing with his wife, Melanie. Except not much vacationing had taken place—not with a computer game that thousands of people around the world depended on him and *only* him to maintain, and four role-playing books that were not going to write themselves. Back in the real world, he held a full-time job. When he had free time, he ate and slept, and even those pesky requirements for functional living had been whittled down to their bare minimums to make more room for everything else.

Biskup looked down at his role-playing books, then glanced over his shoulder at the computer. "I was watching the sun go down over the [Andaman Sea], wondering, *What can I completely give up?* Give up in the sense of, 'No, I'm not going to do this again. It's over. It's really over.'"[1]

Preparing to Climb

For Biskup, born in Germany on July 2nd, 1971, computers and role-playing games went hand in hand. When he was 12, the father of one of his friends worked in the toy department at Karstadt, a mega-chain department store in Germany. Karstadt gave employees a sizeable discount, so one day, Biskup's friend's dad bought a box with *Dungeons & Dragons* written on the front in big, bold letters. Biskup and his friend dug into the box and pored over manuals that showed black-and-white drawings of wizards, warriors, and monsters. *Dungeons & Dragons* was no mere game, they decided. It was a portal to a higher plane.

"I got addicted from the first minute and wanted to have those things for my own. Luckily, my birthday was very soon, so I got the box, too."

Around the same time, Biskup discovered computers. His family owned a Commodore 64 flush with all sorts of games to play. His favorites were sword-and-sorcery fare like *Gates of Apshai* and *The Bard's Tale*, digital adventures that mirrored the pen-and-paper exploits he and his friends acted out while they hunched over card tables in dimly lit rooms.

> There were games like *Sword of Fargoal*, which I really liked to play and had kind of a rogue-like atmosphere. Later on, when I had a PC, I stumbled upon a game called *DND*. It was a random-dungeon exploring game; very primitive, but somehow addictive. I liked it, and that led to my first attempt at writing such a game.

Biskup's infatuation with computer games and programming increased as he grew older. In 1988, he bought an Amiga computer and shelled out a little extra for a disk filled with shareware, demo games that served as samples of full products. His favorite was *Hack*, which displayed dungeons and monsters using text characters instead of crude color graphics.

By 1990, he had enrolled at Technical University of Dortmund and set his sights on a career as a computer scientist. He juggled a full-time course load, but no amount of homework and exams could keep him away from his hobbies. Searching for part-time work, he found a role-playing-game store in need of a designer who could build and maintain a website.

> That was quite disastrous for my financial situation because I put all the money into role-playing games. I had a great chance to get lots of games for little money. I was highly motivated to work a lot because I was paid by the hour. They had demand for web-design stuff, so I worked for many hours and bought many games.

One year into his degree program, Biskup went poking around the university computers and unearthed a game that seemed familiar. It was called *Rogue*, and, like the *Hack* game he had played as a kid, it drafted worlds using letters and symbols. Biskup dug deeper and unearthed *NetHack*, the successor to *Hack*. Time and time again, Biskup failed to finish the game. He admired its scope, but viewed it as needlessly complex and convoluted. Characters like tourists and samurais felt incongruent in a fantasy setting filled with elves, dwarves, and dragons. Worse, there was no story. The goal was to survive and accumulate trinkets rather than develop characters and explore a living, breathing world.

Perturbed, Biskup thought he could invent a more attractive and functional setting. "I thought, *It might be fun to learn a new programming language while I build a better* NetHack. That's how *ADOM* started."

First Steps

Over years of coding homemade games and assignments for programming classes, Biskup had slipped into a comfortable style of development. He liked to start small, implementing one central tenet and building around it as ideas came along. It made sense, then, to learn how to create maps first.

Maps comprised the beating heart of *NetHack* and its ilk. Without interesting maps, players would not feel motivated to fight monsters and search for treasure. Biskup knew that, but encountered a problem. For as rudimentary as drawing maps out of text characters seemed, conceiving the algorithms that drew sinuous hallways, treasure chambers, and great halls was harder than he had thought. Some of his early attempts were the video-game-level equivalent of tangled balls of yarn. Even when his algorithms yielded navigable dungeons, he could not figure out how to calculate line of sight, which restricted the player's already-minimal view.

After several failed attempts, he gave up and doubled down on completing his computer science degree and playing pen-and-paper RPGs. As he wrote code and rolled dice, his failure gnawed at him. Being unable to create procedurally generated maps bothered him not only as a creative person. It bugged him as a computer scientist. Of all the engineering and mathematical mountains he had climbed, only that one seemed insurmountable.

On July 12th, 1994, one year since his last go at writing a roguelike, Biskup returned to the foot of the mountain and scrutinized it.[2] His conclusion was that he had started too big, even though he had intended to do the opposite. Scrapping his old code, he focused on generating small maps first. When this set of algorithms panned out, he added the player-character, the famous "@" symbol, and wrote code necessary to move the famous avatar around. To his delight, he was able to guide the "@" up and down a few simple corridors.

Excited by his progress, Biskup resisted the urge to tack on complexities like twisting passageways. Line-of-sight was still a formidable obstacle, and would become more troublesome if his maps grew too complex too fast. He took things slow, adding a few corridors, then doors so that the "@" could move between rooms. Monsters followed, though they stood immobile, their heads empty of artificial brains. Eager as he was to cut down trolls, orcs, and skeletons, he was determined to test each component before building on top of it.

Biskup's step-by-step approach paid off. In a relatively short time, he got line of sight working, and programmed monsters to patrol hallways. After setting the core mechanics in place, he broadened his algorithm to produce wending dungeons complete with stairs that connected levels. While devising a slate of quests for players to undertake, he realized he was guilty of doing the same thing as the roguelikes he had set out to best. Every mission he crafted involved descending through dungeons and retrieving some bauble. Such simplistic objectives were in contrast to his favorite moments in role-playing campaigns: playing out the consequences his party had made.

Almost by accident, Biskup hit on the concept his game was missing. "I played *Omega*, another of those ancient, almost-forgotten roguelikes. I never got my hands on a properly working version; it was always buggy. But it had this surface world, and I just liked the idea of that."

Omega's surface world captivated Biskup in a way that *Rogue* and *NetHack*'s dungeons could not. Mountains, streams, and forests covered the screen. There were interior regions as well, dungeons teeming with monsters and artifacts, but those environs were side attractions. Players entered subterranean venues, cleared them of monsters and treasure, and returned to the sunlit overworld, *Omega*'s main stage.

Most impressively, *Omega* had an actual plot, and the choices players made along their journey set them on a path to an ending that differed depending on those decisions. That, Biskup resolved, was the type of roguelike game he wanted to make. "I really like a good story, and that was where lots of roguelikes were [lacking]. You had *Rogue* and *NetHack* with their 'go down into the dungeon and find something' stories, which I didn't find too interesting."

To tell compelling stories built around choice and causality, Biskup knew his roguelike needed to play out in a world populated with a multitude of settings: cities, lakes, rivers, oceans, temples, rolling hills, and mountains.

Collectively, the many locations he created would be known as Ancardia, the setting of the *Ancient Domains of Mystery*.

Corruption and Quests

Years of rolling dice and filling out character sheets had taught Biskup a pivotal lesson: the first step to getting players excited about an adventure was encouraging them to bond with their characters. Therefore, the first thing players got to do in *Ancient Domains of Mystery*—which Biskup referred to as *ADOM*—was define a character to their liking. First, players selected their gender. Then they moved on to finer details such as race and class. Over the years, Biskup would add more than 10 races and 20 classes totaling over 200 combinations.

Players inherited skills that hinged on the race and class they chose. Fighters and Paladins were both competent warriors, but Paladins had an edge in casting divine spells. A Priest could cast more complex divine magic than his Paladin brethren. Trolls recovered from wounds faster than other races but needed more food to stay nourished. Gray Elves were haughty and had a mean streak, but were the most magically proficient. Sturdier races were able to wear heavier armor and wield bigger weapons, while smaller races were nimbler.

For all the doors closed by certain race/class combinations and opened by others, Biskup made it a point to let players learn how to use any weapon they found. To his thinking, anyone in the real world could learn how to wield a sword given enough time and training, even though some would be more adroit than others. In *ADOM*, Wizards may never swing a sword as expertly as Fighters, but there is nothing to stop from them from becoming proficient enough to defend themselves if and when their magic runs dry.

After defining their characters, players got their first glimpse of Ancardia. Made up of dozens of individual locations, Ancardia had been invaded by forces of Chaos. Chaos affected players in numerous ways. Triggering a corruption trap infected the player, as did taking damage from corruption-infused monsters, eating corrupted corpses, activating Chaos artifacts, and imbibing certain potions. Venturing into an area where Chaos hangs in the air like a miasma caused unpredictable mutations. The ultimate goal of *ADOM* was to seal the cracks through which Chaos has been flooding in, returning Ancardia to normal.

Allowing players to become tainted simply by spending time in Chaos-heavy areas was Biskup's method of keeping them focused on their goal. "To keep players on a path, you need to invent a compelling story. If the story is good enough, interesting enough, challenging enough, people will be motivated to follow it. If it's not good enough, they will leave it."

Chaos is not always detrimental. As players expose themselves to it, weird mutations occur. A hero's cranium may expand to two or three times its normal size, bequeathing an increase to willpower and learning attributes, while appearance and toughness take a hit. Extra eyes may sprout on a hero's face like pimples, granting greater perception. Poison dripping from fingers strengthens melee attacks, but spoils any food or potions the player touches.

Players who desire combustible power can seek out mutations, while players role-playing pure characters like Priests and Paladins may go out of their way to avoid them. But players who desire Chaos must walk a fine line: becoming inculcated by corruption opens up the possibility of seeing *ADOM*'s chaotic ending; taking on too much corruption overwhelms the hero and ends the game.

Cleansing Ancardia of Chaos was the ultimate goal of *ADOM*, but Biskup populated his world with all manner of optional quests. At the beginning of the game, players chose lawful, neutral, or chaotic alignment. Their alignment determined how NPCs reacted to them, and which quests they could accept. Many quests could be solved in several ways, and the methods players employed influenced non-player character (NPC) dispositions. One mission involved traveling to the town of Terinyo and killing a druid who dwelled there. However, the townsfolk revered the druid, so charging in and attacking turned the townsfolk hostile. To keep their reputation intact, players had to kill the druid surreptitiously in a way that could not incriminate them.

Other quests were more straightforward. Just south of Terinyo lay the Infinite Dungeon, a series of descending levels. Deeper levels contained tougher foes and greater treasures. Biskup distinguished the Infinite Dungeon by generating new levels every time a player entered the labyrinth. He estimated that roughly 80 to 90 percent of *ADOM* is procedurally generated. Some regions, such as the village where players begin the quest, are static. Others, such as elemental temples, contain a mix of pre-constructed and procedurally generated content.

As proud as he is of complex systems like villages and cities full of people that react realistically to the player's actions, Biskup confessed that the biggest challenge in writing *ADOM* was creating interactions that felt real to players, and creating a world that reacted to their presence organically.

> One thing I learned from previous experiences is that having many small stories with limited interactions and ways to change them, and then putting them all together—you suddenly get a very real and interesting world. The many small things in and of themselves are easy to understand and control. If they are mixed with, say, not just two storylines, but maybe 20 or 30 are running in parallel—that contributes to an interesting world.

Factoring in a myriad of race and class combinations, plus the way avatars and the world of Ancardia can manipulate one another through mutations, items, and quest outcomes, has forced Biskup to reconcile with the fact that not every game session will end to the player's liking. That, he believes, is one of *ADOM*'s biggest appeals.

> Whatever interaction happens, happens. That might lead to some stories being unwinnable, but that's real life. The hero you need to defeat some evil mastermind gets killed in some other event? Well, you should have moved faster. That's something I liked about Peter Molyneux's original idea for *Fable*: this idea that every action has a consequence.

Magical Moments

Like a sculptor working stone, Biskup chipped away at his algorithms until, a few months after beginning work in 1994, he launched an early prototype, created a character, and set foot in the realm of Ancardia. The experience had a profound effect on him.

> When I started programming it, I was not sure if I was intelligent enough or skilled enough to write such a game. Being able to play and see that it worked was very nice for me. I was very motivated to continue. I thought, *Okay, it's far enough [along] that I know I can turn it into the game I want it to be.*

In January 1996, Biskup took an even bigger step. Now on the web, he located a couple of newsgroups inhabited by roguelike enthusiasts and uploaded version 0.7.0 of *ADOM*. The incipient game had progressed from the crawling stage to tottering on unsteady legs. A single quest was available to play. Elements of the surface map, such as trees, were displayed in color. Monsters behaved intelligently, maneuvering around traps and collecting experience to increase their strength. Shopkeepers were given names and personalities.

Jotting a quick note to members of the rec.games.roguelike.announce and rec.games.roguelike.misc newsgroup communities announcing *ADOM*'s availability, Biskup sat back and waited for feedback to come pouring in. Not a single person responded. For all Biskup knew, no one had tried the game.

Undeterred, he plugged away, fixing bugs, adding a more informative start screen, and adding monsters and items. On February 22, he uploaded version 0.7.1. "Then some person from somewhere in the world said, 'Hey, I downloaded your game and it was great.' That was certainly cool for me, because I thought, *Wow, I have a means to interact with other people in the world.*"

Ecstatic that he was performing for an audience, Biskup went into overdrive, releasing 11 more updates to *ADOM* in 1996.[3] Every new version introduced more items, quests, monsters, and features such as weather effects and encounters with wild animals. More questers ventured into Ancardia with every update.

> It became a motivational process all over again. I loved hearing their ideas and mixing them with my ideas, and getting them into the game, surprising people with them. That was the point when the Internet allowed us to communicate much easier.

ADOM climbed to new heights when the game captured the number 30 slot on the Internet Worldcharts for Free Games, a listing of the most popular free-to-download games as voted by users.[4] Week by week, month by month, *ADOM* scaled the rankings, reaching the top 20 and ascending even higher to the top 10, then the top 5. Finally, Dan Shiovitz, an avid RPG player and programmer, created a newsgroup for *ADOM*: rec.games.roguelike.adom. Biskup was elated. Only the most popular games like *Rogue* and *NetHack* warranted a dedicated repository of information.

In 1997, *ADOM* and Biskup finally reached the zenith when the game was voted the best free downloadable game of the year. He was speechless. Biskup had never charged money for *ADOM*. On his website, he wrote that donations were welcome but never necessary nor expected. The appreciation and heady flight of his game to the top of the mountain was reward enough. Biskup's fans disagreed, and showed their appreciation in a more unique way. "I thought, *There's no money in [ADOM], but it might be nice to get postcards for all over the world from people I would never meet otherwise.* I love to be surprised by a postcard in my post box by someone somewhere in the world."

Biskup lost count of his postcards years ago, though he estimates his collection to be in the thousands. Some are of the generic "Wish you were here!" variety that one finds in souvenir shops. Others are more specialized, such as one carved from wood. Another came from Antarctica. Opening his post box one afternoon, he found a wedding invitation from a couple he had never met. Another was poster-sized. When a large box arrived on his doorstep, he found over 50 assorted postcards.

In the mid-1990s, Biskup received perhaps his most moving set of fan mail. The missives came from residents caught in the crossfire of the Yugoslav Wars, a series of conflicts that occurred when Yugoslavia splintered into republics. Each republic declared independence, but minorities such as Albanians and Serbs did not have representation in the new governments that sprang up. As a result, horrific crimes against humanity transpired, including ethnic cleansings and the proliferation of rape camps.

"During the war, I got postcards from people in Yugoslavia who said, 'Thank you so much for your game,' Biskup said. "'It allows us to get a little bit of happiness in very dark times. We can play it on our old computers.' That meant a lot to me. To know there's someone in a war region, probably suffering, who gets a little enjoyment from my game—that affected me in a huge way."

Lapses

Biskup had never aspired to get paid for making games. The video-game industry had matured rapidly in Japan and the United States, but grew slowly in Germany. As far as he knew, finding gainful employment programming games was not even an option.

What he really wanted to do was be in the Internet business. The advent of the World Wide Web had made it possible for *ADOM* to reach thousands of people across the world. With more companies planting stakes in Internet soil every day, there would be no lack of opportunities for driven programmers. In 1998, he graduated cum laude from Technical University of Dortmund. He considered starting a software development company, but concluded that he lacked the experience to pilot a one-man enterprise. Instead, he applied to a web company, PRO DV Software AG, and was brought on as a software architect in the summer of '98, where he wrote frameworks in Java, one of the languages taking the Web by storm.

Like so many roguelike authors, Biskup found that maintaining full-time employment and personal relationships took a toll on writing games.

> When I started developing *ADOM*, I did it during my time as a student. I was a decent student, so I had a lot of spare time. I was programming *ADOM* fanatically. I spent many, many hours of the day working on *ADOM*, mostly night hours. Other real-life intrusions also happened during that time. I suddenly had to learn that I had less time to work on *ADOM* in the way I was accustomed to.

In November 1998, Biskup released one update for *ADOM*, version 0.9.9 Gamma 12. The update was incremental, meant to tidy up odds and ends like bugs that crashed the game in odd circumstances. In early June 1999, he rolled out two sizeable updates that squashed bugs where the game broke in specific circumstances, such as players becoming trapped in a casino or digging rivers underground as a new means of ingress to certain areas.

The next update came six months later. In his online journal, Biskup admitted that his time and interest in maintaining *ADOM* had waned due to other commitments. A sudden resurgence in *NetHack*'s development rekindled his passion for his project, and he promised himself that he would push harder toward his next big milestone: version 1.0.0.

Development on *ADOM* went dark for 20 months. Then, in August 2001, Biskup emerged and uploaded version 1.0.0. Exhausted but pleased, he professed that he still had a lot of work to do, but was thrilled to have come so far with so little free time. In November 2002, Biskup uploaded version 1.1.0 followed swiftly by 1.1.1. They were his last updates for nine years.

Like a tidal wave, professional responsibilities crashed over Biskup. He had thrown in with two colleagues to found a company, Quinscape GmbH. As managing director, he was in charge of facilitating relationships with the firm's customers. During long hours, he would have flashes of inspiration for new features and fixes for *ADOM*, but by the time he got home, he was too tired to write code.

In 2011, Biskup traveled to Thailand for holiday. He brought along the four RPG books he was writing, clinging to the one hobby for which he still had time. One evening, as the sun sank into the Andaman Sea, he took stock and realized that his adult responsibilities left room for only one passion project: writing RPG books that might one day sit on bookshelves next to *Dungeons & Dragons* manuals, or maintaining *ADOM*. For a brief, agonizing instant, he considered cutting ties with Ancardia.

> Then I realized: no. Why give that up? There are so many cool people out there. I set a goal of doing a release on my birthday. That was somehow motivating to say, 'Let's try to do this.' I was lucky that my wife was very understanding. That was just a cool moment because suddenly the thing flared back into life. I rekindled my love for programming, gave up the other hobbies, and focused again on *ADOM*.

Crowd Support

Over the nine years that *ADOM* lay dormant, Biskup did not follow in the footsteps of Michael Toy, Robert Koeneke, and the developers of *NetHack* and *Angband*. Since laying the first tile in Ancardia, Biskup had thought of *ADOM* as more than a programming exercise. It was a living, breathing world—*his* world. He would not hand it over to someone who might sully it by adding content that did not fit in with its stories and themes.

Biskup also found the idea of variants based on his source code off-putting. He worried that players who downloaded an offshoot of *ADOM* would connect the variant to him and bombard his inbox with pleas for help fixing bugs or understanding how to play.

Biskup did not covet his source code out of greed or pride. One of the joys of playing roguelikes is discovering some new tactic, item, or special effect brought on by worshipping at an altar or drinking an untested potion, and sharing the experience with fellow players on newsgroups and message boards. To him, giving away *ADOM*'s source code would be tantamount to a magician giving away trade secrets for free.

Jochen Terstiege was the one exception to Biskup's rule. They had met at university, and became colleagues years later. With Biskup's consent and approval, Terstiege had ported the source code to the Amiga, as well as BeOS, Windows, and Mac OS X. In 2010, Terstiege approached Biskup with an announcement. "He said, 'I've been doing some experiments with *ADOM*, and it looks like you could compile it for the iPad.' It didn't look very charming, but you could compile it at least," Biskup recalled.

Porting *ADOM* to the Apple iPad intrigued Biskup. Flocks of games landed on Apple's App Store daily, and some developers were making enough to support themselves. Biskup and Terstiege researched what it took to launch a successful mobile app. The answer was apparent, yet overwhelming. Long-time roguelike players accepted—and even preferred—text-based graphics because many of them had been playing *Rogue* and its descendants since the 1980s. Text-based interfaces were what they knew, and had become a staple of the roguelike formula. But gamers brought up on a steady diet of smartphones and tablets would expect flashier presentation. Moreover, Biskup was rusty at writing code. He had been managing employees for years, and needed to brush up before he returned to the trenches.

What he needed, for the first time in *ADOM*'s history, was a DevTeam. "I noticed this crowdfunding stuff becoming mainstream. I said, 'If we really want to do more than just a tech demo, we needed to put more effort behind it.' Crowdfunding seemed to be a way [to do] that."

Biskup formulated a plan. He and Terstiege would handle coding. For sophisticated artwork and a collection of music and sound effects, he turned to his online community. Krzysztof Dycha had entered a design competition for *ADOM II*, a graphics-driven sequel that Biskup had begun under the name *JADE* (*Java-based Ancient Domains Engine*). Biskup had chosen Dycha as the winner out of dozens of entries. He had been similarly impressed by sound samples sent in by Oneiros Dieguez, and enlisted Dieguez as his composer.

On July 2nd, 2012, Biskup's 41st birthday, *ADOM*'s crowd-funding campaign went live on Indiegogo, a platform where users pledge money toward a product or service in exchange for rewards such as t-shirts and software. Biskup spread the news across newsgroups, Web forums, and other pockets of the Internet where roguelike and *ADOM* fans gathered. He shot a video for the campaign from his inner sanctum: a guesthouse lined with bookshelves bearing the loads of RPG guidebooks, action figures, computer games, and knick-knacks he had amassed over the years.

His goal was an all-or-nothing attempt to resurrect development of *ADOM* and *ADOM II*. To work around his full-time job, he needed to raise $48,000 in 60 days—all of which would fund development and pay his team. Donors could pledge $10 to get their name listed in the credits of *ADOM*'s manual, or pay more to receive special pre-release builds of the game as Biskup and his team rolled them out. If he came up even a dollar short, the campaign would fail, and all donations would be returned.

Biskup's schedule changed once the Indiegogo clock began ticking. Normally, he got up at 6:00 a.m., worked between 10 and 12 hours, got home around 8:00, and spent time with Melanie before going to bed. Managing the campaign and renewing work on *ADOM* added several hours to his schedule. He got up an hour earlier, worked on *ADOM* and *ADOM II* for a few hours before heading into work, got home at the same time, returned to the computer, spent an hour or two with Melanie, then stumbled into bed around midnight.

At first, the long hours paid off. Several thousand dollars poured in during the first week as *ADOM* fans converged on the campaign page, expressing excitement that Biskup had woken the beloved game from its long hibernation. A week later, a setback stalled the campaign.

> There was one magical and bitter moment when someone tried to buy the highest bidding level. That was very motivating. And then, due to technical problems, it failed to happen [because the payment did not go through]. That was a letdown. I felt destroyed for a couple of days.

Whether because most crowdfunding campaigns usually blast off like a rocket then fizzle after the excitement of the first few days, or because of the technical snafu that impeded the big payment, *ADOM*'s Indiegogo page became a ghost town. Biskup redoubled his efforts, blogging, posting screenshots from the set of graphics that would be implemented if the project achieved funding, stopping by roguelike haunts, and providing updates on social media. The needle did not budge.

> I started to wonder, *Will this be successful?* There was quite a bit of criticism from a very loud number of people. That was quite challenging emotionally. I was constantly wondering if we would even be successful. We were thinking of all sorts of ways to motivate people.

His grassroots efforts paid off. With only one week left, *ADOM* hit its funding goal. Biskup immediately began promoting stretch goals, additional funding markers that showered donors with perks at certain intervals: painterly graphics at $55,000; additional races and classes if the campaign reached the $60,000 marker; and sets of quests at $75,000, with more quests added for every additional $5,000 raised—all the way through a version of the game for Android systems at $130,000.

Biskup, his team, and *ADOM* fans were not the only ones invested in the outcome.

> In the last 24 hours, we earned something like one-third of the funding amount. My wife hardly slept during that time, either. We were sitting in front of the computer just watching.

It was a totally amazing experience, and totally draining. Luckily that was on a Friday, so all I had to do was get something to eat and drink when the campaign succeeded, and then we got some sleep.

Seeing Melanie as excited as he was for *ADOM* to return thrilled Biskup. She was a writer, and not on the friendliest of terms with computers; her involvement with them extended as far as writing. To her, playing and writing games was her husband's weird hobby. Unbeknownst to Biskup, his fundraising campaign changed her perspective.

The magical moment was when I saw a donation from her, without her telling me. I think that was a turning point for her. She realized, oh, there are thousands of people out there interested in this. She knew a little bit about the history of *ADOM*, but we didn't know each other when *ADOM* was at its most successful. I think it was interesting for her to see all that stuff happening.

Looking to the Future

All tallied, Biskup raised $90,169 when the campaign clock expired on August 30th, 2012.[5] Since revivifying *ADOM*, he and his team have been turning out regular updates to both *ADOM* and *ADOM II*. With *ADOM II*, Biskup hopes to address some of the complaints his fans have leveled at him over the years. Many players find the story interesting, but do not care to be prodded along by the internal clock that afflicts characters with corruption, believing roguelikes are best savored rather than devoured. While *ADOM*'s main quest will retain the focus on driving players to clear Chaos before they capitulate, Biskup plans to give players more freedom to play *ADOM II* at their own pace.

He also hopes to lower the barrier of entry for players interested in trying the original *ADOM*.

For example, one thing we discussed today was whether it might be a good idea to remove traps while you're a level-1 character. The traps in *ADOM* are very dangerous, and the [level of danger] doesn't seem quite right. So maybe it's a better idea to just do away with them for the first level. Most players probably wouldn't even notice if there weren't any traps while they're [playing] level-1 characters.

No matter what the future brings, one tenet of Anrcadia will never change.

I have to say I've never done *ADOM* for the money because there's not much money in it, even with the crowdfunding campaign. I'm really doing it because I love playing this type of game and programming this type of game. Everything else is a bonus. If people love it, so much the better.

* * *

Side Quests

Creator's Day

Biskup celebrated his decision to resurrect *ADOM* development by releasing version 0.1.0 of *JADE*, short for *Java-based Ancient Domains Engine*, also known as *ADOM II*, a graphical successor to his original game, on July 2nd, 2011. Biskup's birthday is known to fans as Creator's Day and is celebrated by players around the world.

Notes

1. I was watching the sun go down over the ocean: Interview with Thomas Biskup. All quotes from Thomas Biskup come from interviews conducted between 2012 and 2014.
2. On July 12th, 1994: "Technical Stuff 'N' Statistics." *Ancient Domains of Mystery*. http://www.adom.de/adom/history.php3.
3. Ecstatic that he was performing for an audience: Ibid. (Author's note: From this point on in the chapter, I refrained from citing dates on which updates to *ADOM* were released, since they can easily be found on the *ADOM* history page.)
4. *ADOM* climbed to new heights: "I.D. Licensing ADOM and other commercial ventures." *The ADOM Fluff FAQ*. http://web.mit.edu/yoz/adom/readme.1st. (Author's note: Worldcharts.com is now defunct.)
5. All tallied, Biskup raised: "Resurrect ADOM Development." *Indiegogo.com*. https://www.indiegogo.com/projects/resurrect-adom-development.

10

The Future of Play

It's true that *Rogue* will very likely never come up in conversation between casual gamers who feel more comfortable sticking to yearly iterations of *Call of Duty* and *Assassin's Creed*. However, it's also true that roguelike trappings have left their mark on some of the most popular mainstream games. Enter the roguelike-like, a type of game influenced by roguelike systems such as permadeath and procedural generation, but not strictly a roguelike.

Matthew Davis and Justin Ma are the co-creators of *FTL: Faster Than Light*, an indie game where players board a spaceship, travel through space, battle enemy ships, and experience procedural content such as exploding stars that force the player to make careful, tactical decisions. One wrong move, and permadeath rears its ugly yet oddly enticing head.

In 2012, I interviewed Ma and Davis for a short book entitled *Anything But Sports: The Making of FTL*. Davis speaks to the emphasis he and Ma placed on death as a learning tool when they drafted their list of features for the game. "I think games have lost the idea that dying matters. Which was actually all that [I wrote] down: 'Dying matters,' this concept that dying does punish the player."[1]

Justin Ma agrees: "When you're making these decisions, if there isn't this sense of impending doom and pressure from making mistakes, there isn't as much impact. We knew we needed to have permadeath."[2]

The rise of *FTL* caused many members of the games press to label it a roguelike, which in turn sparked debate within the roguelike community: what is the defining element, the *sine qua non*, of a roguelike? Is it the presence of procedural generation? Permadeath? Turn-based gameplay? Text-based graphics?

Respected members of the roguelike community weighed in. Darren Grey, co-founder and co-host of the Roguelike Radio podcast, argues that the definition of the genre should be flexible.

> Turn-based play isn't necessary to make a roguelike, I believe. I enjoy those mechanics, but some games have played with that. For instance, *FTL* is real-time, but lets you pause and give commands at any point. That actually works really well. It gives you a complete roguelike feeling, a control over time.

Besides incorporating permadeath and procedural generation, Davis and Ma saw the advantage in giving players time to sort through all possible decisions and their consequences. Ma acknowledged that for some reason, if you pump up the intensity but you [are allowed to] pause the game, it's still a very intense experience. You can pause the game and stare at everything, and still your heart is pumping because you can see all these problems. While it's paused, you have time to consider, like making a chess move.

Davis and Ma were no strangers to roguelike games when they set out to write *FTL*. They appreciated the genre, but did not expect any game carrying its DNA to make a splash in mainstream circles. Roguelikes, and roguelike-likes, were punishing, as infamous for scaring players away as for providing deep gameplay experiences unlike those in any other type of game. To say *FTL* defied the odds and their expectations would be a gross understatement. Twenty-four hours after launching a crowdfunding campaign on Kickstarter, set at $10,000—the amount they needed to finish the game—they had raised $20,000. They rode that momentum to a windfall of more than $200,000 and wave after wave of positive coverage that lasted through the game's release in 2012.

"The game's random nature ensures that while there's a singular objective in your sights, all the way at the other side of the sector map, what you're really doing is telling a new story every time," writes *Eurogamer* editor Dan Whitehead in his review of the game. "It's the very definition of a game that is all about the journey rather than the destination."[3]

Blizzard Entertainment's *Diablo* series—created at the now-defunct Blizzard North studio—is inarguably the most popular example of roguelike systems writ large in mainstream gaming. While speaking to him for my *Stay Awhile and Listen* series of books, Blizzard North co-founder David Brevik explained that he thought up the premise of *Diablo* after immersing himself in roguelikes during his college years.

> Roguelikes always convey an overall goal for what you're trying to do. In *Moria*, you have to kill a Balrog or something. So you work on making your way down, and the game gets harder and harder as you go down. It's a very simple game concept. Everybody understands that as you go further down, the game gets harder. Just saying, 'Hey, there's a bad guy down on level 20' or whatever was easy to convey to players.[4]

Diablo started out as an homage to roguelikes: a single-player, turn-based RPG with procedurally generated dungeons and weapons, but with graphics instead of text characters. At the behest of the principals at Blizzard Entertainment, *Diablo*'s publisher, the Blizzard North team stripped away the genre's esoteric trappings, leaving a graphical, real-time game that could be played solely by clicking a mouse. No keyboard required. "So easy your mom can play it" was the guiding manifesto that influenced every design decision made by the Blizzard North team

As much fun as millions of players had clicking their way down through dungeons, procedural generation made up the core of *Diablo* and drove the game to the top of bestseller lists "Fundamentally, roguelikes are about randomness, so having the random levels was always a key concept to replayability. That's what we wanted first and foremost: a game you could play over and over again that would be different every time," says Brevik in *Stay Awhile and Listen: Book I*.

Blizzard Entertainment's principals agreed with Brevik and his two co-founders, Max and Erich Schaefer, that generating levels would be instrumental to the game's success. Selling them on the virtues of permadeath was an uphill battle. Brevik relayed his passion for the mechanic to me in our interviews.

> Part of the way a turn-based game becomes compelling and exciting is when you're done to your last few hit points, you're up against a tough monster, you have a bunch of things you can do, and you're sitting there thinking about it. You're like, 'Should I use this potion? Should I swing at this guy? What should I do, here? If I make the wrong choice, my guy's dead. I've spent twelve hours building this guy, I haven't slept tonight, and I'm going to make a bad choice right now.' And you do. You do, and you die, and you cry all night or all day, and then you come back and play again.

Blizzard Entertainment refused to budge: permadeath had no place in *Diablo*. For *Diablo II*, released in 2000, Blizzard North and Blizzard Entertainment reached a compromise. Hardcore, a mode of play where characters could only die once, would become available after players had completed the game with a regular, revivable character.

Erich Schaefer stated bluntly that he was an advocate of permadeath.

> We made Hardcore happen, and everybody loved it, but there was controversy, especially from Blizzard South, thinking that once [players] actually died, they'd hate us, hate Blizzard, hate *Diablo*. But we kept fighting back, saying, 'No, they'll know what they're getting into. Yeah, dying will suck, but it will add a lot of excitement for some people.' I think it was a great decision.[5]

Players and members of the gaming press agreed. "Let me put this as simply as I can," wrote *GameSpot* editor Alex Sassoon on May 14th, 2012, two days after the release of the highly anticipated *Diablo III*.

> If you're playing *Diablo III* and not playing Hardcore, you're doing it wrong. [...] It's more challenging, it's more exciting, and, above all, it's just more fun. You have no idea how attached you can get to a character until you've gone through 90 levels of Hardcore *Diablo II* with them, battling bosses [and] fleeing from lightning-charged cow kings. *Diablo III* is gloomy and atmospheric, but the tension only becomes real when death carries a penalty. Actual jeopardy is nearly non-existent in games these days; we've been coddled with auto-saves, checkpointing, and infinite lives, and gaming is the poorer for it.[6]

During a Reddit AMA (Ask Me Anything) conducted with game designers from Blizzard Entertainment in early June 2012, just a few weeks after the release of *Diablo III*, senior designer Wyatt Chang released statistics on the percentage of players going through the game as Hardcore characters. "The data I have on hand is from yesterday, at which time 4.1% of the characters are made in Hardcore."[7]

On its own, 4.1 percent may seem a trivial amount. But consider the math Chang used to reach that conclusion. On day one of *Diablo III*'s availability on PC, Blizzard announced that 4.7 *million* players logged on to Battle.net to play the game.[8] One week later, Blizzard had sold 6.3 million units.[9] By July, "more than 10 million people [had] played *Diablo III*."[10]

Since the Reddit AMA took place approximately one month before *Diablo III* hit its 10 million player base, we'll round down a little and presume that around 7 million players had logged on around the time of the AMA. Per Chang's numbers, 4.1 percent of 7 million works out to 287,000 players—a nontrivial number, and one that grew in the months and years following. "Hardcore is a super exciting way to play so it's very important to us. We take into account Hardcore for every design decision," Chang confirmed during the AMA.

Procedural generation and permadeath are not just popular among players. Developers have embraced them, too. Ido Yehieli is the creator of *Carinal Quest*, a roguelike game that strips out more complex systems such as unwieldy control schemes so that players can concentrate on exploration and combat. Yehieli was drawn to roguelikes because of the genre's focus on gameplay over graphics. "It seemed like something I could do by myself compared to all the other games I was playing at the time, like *StarCraft*, which I had no clue how to make," he told me.[11]

Procedural generation gives programmers more freedom to focus on systems. In a linear game with set, static levels, a game system may break down if players cannot use it effectively in a certain area. An even more nightmarish scenario: designers could decide to scrap or overhaul a system, rendering level architecture built with that system in mind worthless. But procedural games craft different areas every time, forcing players to change up strategies and taking the pressure off of level designers.

Equally compelling, generating content procedurally translates to game assets that can be reused. For *Diablo*, Blizzard North's artists concentrated on making dozens of tiles showing stone floors and walls. From there, the algorithms took over, rearranging tiles in different ways every time, and eliminating the burden of crafting static levels dependent on specific gameplay. "I think every designer now has to ask themselves, at the start of any game project these days, 'Is there any way I can procedurally generate any of my content without the quality suffering enormously?' Any answers to the affirmative must be taken seriously. The value-to-cost ratio is just too high," said Tanya X. Short, developer of roguelike-like *Shattered Planet*, in an interview for *Gamasutra* editor Christian Nutt's "'Roguelikes': Getting to the Heart of the It-genre" article published in 2014.[12]

Nutt named his article well. Pull up the Steam digital distribution platform, run a search for roguelike games, and you'll pull up over a dozen pages of search results, all sortable by tags such as "Perma Death" and "Procedural Generation."[13] More than *Rogue*, more than *NetHack*, more than *Diablo*, the powerful and flexible systems conceived in roguelike games are driving innovation in games—and will continue to do so for years to come.

"A game is basically content that you churn through, and I think video and computer games are a much more profound thing than that," says John Harris, a roguelike historian and author of the *@Play* series of articles that explore the finer points of roguelike design.

> Exploring rules to produce very deep games that keep players interested for a very long time—that's really what *Rogue* is about. Exploring those rules through procedural generation, simple rules with profound consequences—not just roguelikes, but all games are basically that.[14]

Rogue. Moria. NetHack. ADOM. These and the other roguelikes chronicled across the pages of *Dungeon Hacks* originated on gigantic computers that have long since been unplugged and donated to museum exhibits. Yet the roguelikes conceived on those systems persist—and they disprove the notion that video games must boast state-of-the-art graphical technology to capture interest.

Angband has thrived since its inception in the 1990s. Thomas Biskup and his small team have been rolling out new versions of *ADOM* and *ADOM II* since the culmination of his Indiegogo crowdfunding campaign. Both games boast updated graphical veneers, although players who swear by text-based graphics can switch over to the familiar overlay of hash symbols, dashes, and "@" signs if they so desire.

NetHack, dormant for over 12 years, is due to receive an update—the first since version 3.4.3 released in December 2003. "Despite a lot of opinions to the contrary, we aren't dead and we haven't given up on the game," DevTeam founder Mike Stephenson wrote on nethack.org in April 2015.[15] True to form, he declined to specify a release date.

> To do so would break a long-standing *NetHack* tradition, but there is a more important reason. Given the amount of time since the previous release, and considering what's been integrated into it, knocking the bugs out of it may not be as easy an exercise as in the past, so we're loath to commit to a date and have something throw us off.

News of *NetHack*'s resurrection stirred Internet forums into a frenzy. Every update to *Angband* and *ADOM* is met with excitement. Players flock to message boards to swap stories of "Yet Another Stupid Death," and to post screenshots of narrowly won (or lost) battles down in the deepest, darkest dungeons.

If you were new to the roguelike scene, you would be forgiven for asking why. Why do these games, with their primitive graphics, inscrutable systems, and punishing consequences continue to thrive more than 35 years after their origination?

One reason is immunity to ageism. Hardware is inherently and inexorably anchored to Moore's Law. In 1965, Intel co-founder Gordon Moore predicted that technology would double its capabilities every two years. That ultra-fast, ultra-expensive microprocessor or graphics card you scrimp and save for today will run games at a crawl in a few years or less. Moore's Law has long dictated hardware shifts in the games industry. From the 1980s through the 2000s, Sony, Microsoft, Nintendo, and Sega released new game consoles every four to five years in a bid to hold the attention of consumers tempted by newer, shinier boxes. Games lauded as technological marvels in their heyday now appear antiquated. Historians and diehard fans still play them, but the mainstream public moves on year by year, console by console.

Even compared to early video games like *Pong*, *Pac-Man*, and *Space Invaders*, the graphics in *Rogue* were rudimentary at best. Yet historians such as Harris argue that *Rogue* was never intended as a graphical showpiece.

> You don't hear as much about it, but in some ways, *Rogue* is still the best roguelike because its different systems fit together the best. It's a game designed in such a way that you can't rely on any one thing. You can find an item that puts one part of the game completely out of play. You can find a ring of slow digestion, and food never becomes a factor. But you do want to put on other rings. No one item will make *Rogue* an instant win because almost all of the items are random.

Moreover, graphics can pose a distraction. Adventure games like *Full Throttle*, *Gabriel Knight: Sins of the Fathers*, and *Maniac Mansion* were celebrated in the 1990s, but even the most ardent players commiserated over pixel hunts, the need to click on a specific pixel hidden in a densely packed background in order to progress.

Angband and *NetHack* may require you to know what a "/" represents versus a "*," but once you decipher the symbols, your imagination, a graphics card that never becomes obsolete, fills in the rest, generating a gameplay-driven experience that never goes out of style.

Harris's enthusiasm for *Rogue* hits on the central reason why classic roguelikes live on: complex, interconnected systems. Many games, especially those predicated on telling a story, are analogous to amusement park rides. You follow a carefully constructed path, leaning into twists and loops engineered to move you along at a deliberate speed. And then the ride is over. You could go another round, but that sense of nervous anticipation as your carriage clanks slowly up a hill, the sight of the park spread out far below you, the rush of exhilaration as the carriage plunges down and shoots you through twists and turns—those can only be experienced for the first time once.

In *Angband* and other roguelikes, player agency—the player's ability to interact with the game world, and the extent to which he or she can manipulate it—feeds into procedural content generation to create a brand new experience each and every time. Erik Osheim, a member of *Angband*'s DevTeam, describes one of his favorite tales of player agency.

> There's someone who famously starts out with no weapons or torch. He goes down blind into the dungeon and finds everything he needs. In some ways, that's kind of a gimmick because you just keep doing that, dying over and over until you stumble on a torch. But if you come up with any challenge, there's probably a player who can do it.[16]

Harris opines that "the better [roguelike games] make you rely on what you find a lot more. You're not guaranteed to find the good stuff in order, or you might find the really good stuff early, or you might have to do without it because you never find it."

Additionally, roguelikes can appear to be sentient. That is precisely what endears the genre to Grey.

> For me, it's about a playable, thinking game, almost a board game-y feel where it's fresh every time you play. Procedural content does that. Permadeath ties in with procedural content because it forces you to restart all the time and forces you to see the procedural elements of the game.[17]

Of course, procedural content is not the end-all, be-all factor. Players can slay as many monsters as they like in *Rogue*, but extra layers of challenge—such as food to prevent starvation—add to the genre's potential for inexhaustible gameplay possibilities. "You don't have an infinite amount of time to explore this space, and that's what makes the dungeon meaningful," Harris explained.

> If it was just a space you moved around in at no cost, it's not interesting. But if there's something, some time limit, something that forces you to explore efficiently—that's interesting. Solving impromptu puzzles, figuring out the most efficient and safest way to explore a space—that's interesting. Also, the items you find, the random resources with which to

explore the space and overcome the dangers. All these systems working together are what make [roguelikes] interesting.

Harris and Grey are fervent supporters of roguelikes, but the mainstream is taking notice of these esoteric adventures, too. In 2012, *TIME* magazine editor Lev Grossman listed *NetHack* as one of the periodical's All-TIME 100 Video Games.

> The character classes alone give you a sense of the game's depth: you can play as an archeologist, a barbarian, a caveman, a knight, a samurai, a Valkyrie, a tourist, or half a dozen other options. *NetHack* is a demanding game — its difficulty and quirkiness have kept it a cult phenomenon — but it's more compelling than most of the chip-melting, big-budget graphical RPGs being released now.[18]

Grossman makes a fair point. Roguelikes will never fall out of vogue for the hardest of hardcore players who commune on message boards and write new flavors of *Angband* for fun.

As for the argument that classic roguelikes will never gain a foothold due to their inherent difficulty, Harris argues that players should not let that deter them.

> Games aren't jobs. The way to enjoy roguelikes is to just play. If you enjoy it, fine. If not, maybe they're not for you. Once you get into them, though, there's so much there, and it's about the experience you have before you die. It's like, 'Okay, this is going well. This is very interesting—and I just died. But before I died, things were very interesting. I died in unexpected places.' If you can get into that and think of roguelikes as random story generators, where you're the protagonist of a story of your own making, that's awesome. I don't know of any genre of game that does it better than roguelikes.

Notes

1. I think games have lost the idea that dying matters: Interview with Matthew Davis. All quotes from Matthew Davis come from interviews conducted from 2012–2014 via email and Skype.
2. When you're making these decisions, if there isn't this sense of impending doom: Interview with Justin Ma. All quotes from Justin Ma come from interviews conducted from 2012–2014 via email and Skype.
3. The game's random nature ensures that while there's a singular objective: "FTL: Faster Than Light review." *Eurogamer.* http://www.eurogamer.net/articles/2012-09-21-ftl-faster-than-light-review.
4. Roguelikes always convey an overall goal for what you're trying to do: Interview with David Brevik. All quotes from David Brevik come from interviews conducted from 2009–2014.
5. We made Hardcore happen, and everybody loved it: Interview with Erich Schaefer. All quotes from Erich Schaefer come from interviews conducted from 2009–2014.
6. Let me put this as simply as I can: "If You're Not Playing Diablo III Hardcore, You're Doing It Wrong." *GameSpot.com.* http://www.gamespot.com/articles/if-youre-not-playing-diablo-iii-hardcore-youre-doing-it-wrong/1100-6376560/.
7. The data I have on hand is from yesterday: "I am (we are) Wyatt Cheng, Andrew Chambers, and Jay Wilson, game designers for Diablo III. AMAA!" *Reddit.com/r/Diablo.* http://www.reddit.com/r/Diablo/comments/uoooj/i_am_we_are_wyatt_cheng_andrew_chambers_and_jay/c4x6s9t.
8. One week later, Blizzard had sold 6.3 million units: "Diablo III Breaks PC Sales Records." *GameInformer.com.* http://www.gameinformer.com/b/news/archive/2012/05/23/diablo-iii-crushes-pc-sales-records.aspx.

9. Ibid.

10. By July, "more than 10 million people [had] played *Diablo III*,": "Diablo III has More Than 10 Million Players." *IGN.com*. http://www.ign.com/articles/2012/08/02/diablo-iii-has-more-than-10-million-players.

11. It seemed like something I could do by myself: Interview with Ido Yehieli. All quotes from Ido Yehieli come from interviews conducted in 2013.

12. I think every designer now has to ask themselves, at the start of every project these days: "'Roguelikes': Getting to the heart of the it-genre." *Gamasutra*. http://www.gamasutra.com/view/feature/218178/roguelikes_getting_to_the_heart_.php.

13. Pull up the Steam digital distribution platform: "Browsing Rogue-like." *Steam*. http://store.steam-powered.com/tag/en/Procedural%20Death%20Labyrinth/#p=0&tab=NewReleases.

14. You don't hear as much about it, but in some ways, *Rogue* is still the best roguelike: Interview with John Harris. All quotes from John Harris come from interviews conducted between 2012 and 2014.

15. Despite a lot of opinions to the contrary: "April 3, 2015 Announcement." *NetHack.org*. http://nethack.org/.

16. There's someone who famously starts out with no weapons or torch: Interview with Erik Osheim. All quotes from Erik Osheim come from interviews conducted during 2014.

17. For me, it's about a playable, thinking game: Interview with Darren Grey. All quotes from Darren Grey come from interviews conducted between 2012 and 2014.

18. The character classes alone give you a sense of the game's depth: "All-TIME 100 Video Games." *Time.com*. http://techland.time.com/2012/11/15/all-time-100-video-games/slide/nethack-1987/.

Rogue's Gallery

Don Worth explores a dungeon in *Beneath Apple Manor*, his groundbreaking dungeon hack for the Apple II. (Photo: Don Worth.)

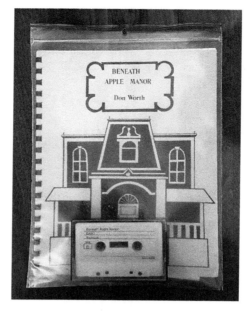

Before big boxes and digital distribution, computer games came on cassette tapes sealed in plastic bags. (Photo: Don Worth.)

Worth gathered up all of his notes, game code, and books, and sent them to an Apple II historian. (Photo: Don Worth.)

"The Stat Lab Gang." Glenn Wichman (bottom, wearing red vest) grows bunny ears courtesy of Michael Toy (top). Toy and Wichman often spent time with the friends they made working in the stat computer lab at University of California Santa Cruz. Leslie "Marty" McNary (bottom, right) was the most devoted of *Rogue*'s play testers. (Photo: Glenn Wichman.)

Michael Toy in the apartment he shared with Glenn Wichman during their time at UCSC. Toy is posing with the ADM-3 computer and 300-baud modem he and Wichman used to dial in to the VAX 11/780 stationed at UCSC, enabling them to write *Rogue* from home. (Photo: Glenn Wichman.)

Toy and Wichman entertain friends in the kitchen of their apartment. From left to right: Wichman (bottom), Toy, Ken Hickman, and Kipp Hickman. (Photo: Glenn Wichman.)

The offices of A.I. Design. Nina Wichman, Glenn's wife, tests the PC version of *Rogue* as Michael Toy looks on. (Photo: Glenn Wichman.)

Epyx loaned Glenn Wichman an Atari ST 1040ST computer, which he used to write the Atari ST version of *Rogue*. (Photo: Glenn Wichman.)

A leprechaun drawn by Glenn Wichman, used for the instruction manual included with the Apple Macintosh version of *Rogue*. (Image: Glenn Wichman.)

An adventurer comes face to face with a troll, and no doubt wishes he had hung a right instead of a left at that last T-junction. This image was drawn by Glenn Wichman for inclusion in the instruction manual for the Macintosh version of *Rogue*. (Image: Glenn Wichman.)

Wichman (left) and Toy cheer on the San Francisco Giants at AT&T Park in 2013. (Photo: Glenn Wichman.)

An excerpt from Jeff McCord's senior yearbook showing his computer teacher, Mike Seiler. (Photo: Jeff McCord.)

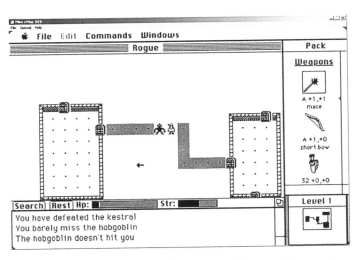

Rogue for the Apple Macintosh. Separate windows contained the main map, which showed the player's immediate surroundings; a minimap that showed the whole level; the player's inventory; and game messages. (Image: Theo Karagiris, TKC8800.com)

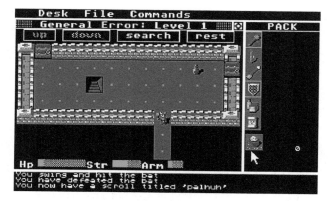

Rogue running on an Atari ST computer. (Image: Mobygames.com.)

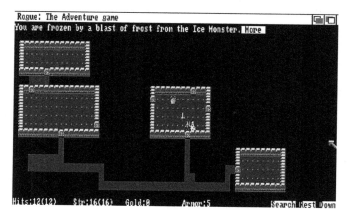

Rogue running on an Amiga computer. (Image: Mobygames.com.)

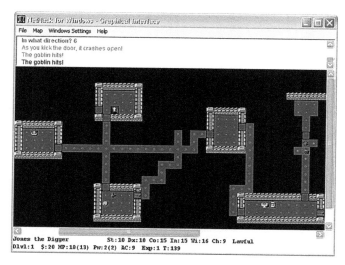

NetHack for Windows paints the text-only interface in color and icons, making the game easier to interpret for new players. (Image: Wikipedia.)

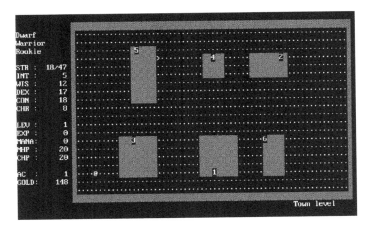

Moria's town, where all players begin their adventures. (Image: Mobygames.)

Bonus Round: Reading, Writing, and Programming—An Interview with Brian Harvey

Some adults look back on high school as the best years of their lives. Others, like me, viewed it like a prison sentence: I went, I did my time, and I got out. Mr. Bill Carli made my four-year sentence much more bearable.

Mr. Carli was my programming teacher, and his computer lab was my home away from home for seven and a half hours every Monday through Friday for four long years—long years made much more bearable thanks to Mr. Carli's kindness. Not that I was an exception. If we needed help with our BASIC, PASCAL, Visual BASIC, or C++ assignments, Mr. Carli squeezed office hours into his schedule. We were even allowed to blast each other to bits in *Unreal* and *Half-Life* after school—provided we kept our grades at a respectable level. Mr. Carli kept the lab open to help kids with their homework, and, I think, because he knew we loved being there as much as he loved having us around.

Teachers can either be rays of sunshine cutting through the darkness, or thunderheads. For me, that ray of sunshine was Mr. Carli. For a tightly knit group of aspiring programmers at Lincoln-Sudbury Regional High School in Lincoln, Massachusetts, it was Brian Harvey.

* *

Could you talk more about the atmospheres of the computer labs at MIT and Stanford, and how they influenced the culture you established at Lincoln-Sudbury?
There were lots of computer labs at MIT, but most of them were encrusted with rules. There was one dedicated to unofficial student projects, but first-semester freshmen weren't allowed to use it, lest we flunk out. Meanwhile I needed the use of a computer to maintain the mailing list of the student radio station WTBS (now called WMBR), and so someone steered me to the Artificial Intelligence Lab. There I was welcomed and had the run of the place.

When I found a bug in TECO, the text editor we used there, and brought it to one of the "real" system programmers, he told me he was busy and I should fix it myself. He showed me how to find the source files and how to run the assembler, then I was on my own to sink or swim. I couldn't believe they'd let a freshman work on the real system programs. Especially one who'd just walked in the door, with no official status. But that's how it was: there *was* no official status. Months later, Richard Greenblatt, a star programmer who terrified me (not intentionally!), walked over to me, stroked his chin, and said, "I guess we ought to start paying you."

I didn't get to Stanford until several years later, as a graduate student. But there too, there was the official computer center, full of rules, and then there was the AI Lab, complete with a few local high school students who'd just wandered in one day and started working on projects. There was one key that opened all the doors at SAIL [Stanford Artificial Intelligence Library], and everyone had a copy.

So when I found myself at Lincoln-Sudbury Regional High School, I knew I wanted to build that kind of environment: one where kids could wander in and just jump into whatever they wanted to work on, not have to jump through hoops. I didn't arrive with the complete vision of the structure we ended up with, but right away I talked the school into letting me not give grades, since I knew that would ruin the freewheeling atmosphere I wanted.

How did you get the position of computer director at the high school?
In the early part of my life I was not at all a people person. I was delighted to spend my time dealing with logical, predictable computers. But after a decade of programming, during which I had started reading books about progressive education, one day I suddenly decided I was bored and wanted to become a progressive teacher. My student teaching experiences made it clear to me that I couldn't work in a rigid, traditional school. I was looking for an alternative or "free" school where I could be a math teacher. (Remember, this was before computers took over the world. It never occurred to me that I could be a teacher of computer programming.)

I had a series of job interviews, in which either the school didn't want me or I didn't want the school. While at Stanford, I had gotten to know Paul Goldenberg, who was then working in the MIT Logo group. I had been telling him and his wife, Cindy Carter, how much trouble I was having finding the kind of school where I wanted to work. Luckily, Paul and Cindy were also friends with Larry Davidson, who happened to tell Paul and Cindy how much trouble he was having finding a candidate for a job setting up a computer department at Lincoln-Sudbury (LS). It was Cindy who had the idea of introducing Larry to me.

I was a little dubious about the job, because LS was a regular old school, not a radically progressive one. But it wasn't oppressive, and the school library had several books by Paul Goodman (one of the theorists of progressive education, and a hero of mine), and the vice principal in charge of discipline talked with me at the interview about sociology rather than about demerits and detentions. So the school and I agreed to take a chance on each other.

I was hired as department head and sole member of a new computer department for two reasons. One is that the math teachers who had set up a computer facility in the math department, Larry Davidson and Phil Lewis, felt that [the computer department] being situated in math might scare off kids who weren't math stars but might still enjoy programming. And the other is that the school was facing layoffs and the rule was last hired first fired within each department. As a newly hired math teacher I would have been gone immediately, but as the sole member of a separate department I was layoff-proof. (I grew up a red diaper baby and a union supporter, so I always felt guilty about that aspect of it.)

Did you encounter much resistance from faculty, administration, and/or parents when you proposed creating an open computer lab where teenagers would be allowed to have (mostly, but not quite totally) free reign over equipment worth thousands of dollars?

Surprisingly little. It really matters that computers were rare back then. It's not like now, when everyone sees programming as a survival skill akin to literacy. I'd never get away with it today, but then computer programming was like art or drama, an elective that wasn't going to get anyone into college or keep them out.

The principal of the school was a businessman by training, not an educator. That sounds terrible, but it was actually great, because his strategy was to hire good people and then let them do what they wanted. He originally wanted me to call it the data processing department and teach business applications like computerized bookkeeping, but he knew that it would be better for me to pursue my vision wholeheartedly than to pursue his miserably.

Other teachers had mixed views. Once the computer center was up and running, you'd open the door of the room and hear kids yelling across the room to their friends and project partners, some kids playing games, some just hanging out, and others hard at work with total concentration. Teachers who thought that in a proper classroom every kid is doing the same thing at the same time, quietly, hated it. But other, more progressive teachers loved it. I was amused that every teacher loved or hated it *instantly*, the moment they walked in, without asking questions.

There were a few kids who didn't like the chaotic feeling either, by the way. In a perfect world I would have had two connected rooms with a big window between them, one of which would be designated the quiet room. You could then be in whichever room you wanted, which might change for the same person at different times.

In those early days, there were teachers who didn't understand what computers could do. I once had an English teacher show up in the computer center very upset because the computer had written a kid's English paper. What that turned out to mean was that the kid used a spelling checker! The teacher ended up happy because this primitive spelling checker didn't actually correct the mistakes, but just pointed them out. The kid then had to find out the old-fashioned way how the word should be spelled. On the other hand, there were teachers who embraced the computer as a teaching tool.

My only real enemy at the school was the administrator of the buildings and grounds staff, who was responsible for school security. He managed to go along with the idea of giving kids keys to the room as long as they were for use during hours when the building was open for business. But once kids started wanting to stay all evening, and come in on the weekends, he had to deal with the presence of kids at times when the corridor doors used to be padlocked shut.

How were you able to swing getting DEC to pay for 75 percent of the mainframe and a bond to cover the remaining 25 percent?

The bond part was just luck. The Massachusetts legislature had just passed a law allowing school boards to issue bonds specifically for computer equipment, and my principal talked the board into using that power.

The DEC grant, though, took a semester of hard work. I wrote the proposal, and we got a sympathetic hearing in part because Sudbury is next door to DEC headquarters in Maynard, and several DEC engineers lived there. But I had many meetings with sales people, technical people, and management people from DEC. (I once almost throttled a kid because he gave me a phone message in the form "someone from DEC called and wants you to call back.")

Of course it helped that I had that decade of programming experience behind me, and a degree from MIT, and experience in particular with DEC products. DEC managers were both skeptical about and intrigued by my ambitious plans, including things like having kids program modifications to the operating system.

What I really wanted was a PDP-10, the machine I'd used at MIT and at Stanford. But I knew they weren't going to give me a half-million-dollar machine, so I asked for a free PDP-11/70, the most powerful model of their minicomputer line. In the end they told me that DEC doesn't like to give 100-percent grants because then people ask for more than they need, but I could have 75 percent off of whatever I wanted.

Could you describe the lab? Was it room filled with dumb terminals connected to a mainframe or minicomputer, as seemed to be common in those days?
We started with six terminals in the computer center, and additional terminals in the library and some administrative offices where kids and staff shared access. (One of the first ways I put kids to work was running RS-232 cable around the building.) Most of the terminals were VT-100 displays, with a few hardcopy terminals added, mainly because they could display the APL character set, and the displays couldn't. We bought a big line printer too.

The PDP-11 was [kept] in a sort of closet next to the computer center, with a connecting door and a big window. When I first arrived, the school had a much smaller PDP-8 system, with hardcopy terminals connected over 20ma lines rather than RS-232. I don't know if you go back far enough to remember 20ma, but it was very sensitive to static electricity, and the school had done the computer lab the favor of putting it in the only carpeted classroom in the school, so there used to be frequent system crashes.

There were three kids who were official assistant managers of the computer back then, and those kids had keys to the inner sanctum. One time when the computer crashed and none of those kids were around, when I had just arrived at the school and had no idea how to restart the computer, another kid stood right at the door giving me instructions.

Me : Why don't you just come in and do it yourself?
Kid : I'm not allowed in there.
Me : Why on earth not?
Kid : Because of that list of everybody's password stuck to the wall.
Me : That's stupid.

And then I took the list and locked it inside the supply cabinet inside the inner room, and declared that anybody could go into the room. For the first few days, kids were coming and going just for the thrill of it. After a while of that I said anyone could come in, but only if they had a real reason. (We hadn't yet invented the idea of making kids make the rules.)
Also, in the inner room was a couch, for use by the three privileged sysadmin [system administrator] kids. I quickly pulled that out to the big room, so that wouldn't be a reason for anyone to be inside. The inner room had been a de facto clubhouse for the sysadmin kids, but I knew the eventual PDP-11 would take up more space, and I didn't want a lot of traffic in there.

These tiny first steps already established my reputation as an educational radical—nothing about teaching or curriculum, just getting rid of stupid reminders to kids how little their wishes counted at school.

I found it interesting that your students went from wanting to hoard software and lock their rivals out of it, to building on the culture you had established by spreading their knowledge far and wide. I know you said you didn't ask or order them to play nicely with others, but I would love to hear more about how the transition happened, from your perspective.

Well, I should say first of all that the change was one of degree, not an overwhelming sudden revolution. There were always kids happy to share, and there were always kids more possessive about their work. I give a lot of the credit to one kid in particular, Robert Brown, who quickly became one of the experts on all aspects of programming, and was, from the beginning, eager to share his understanding with others. He never made anyone feel stupid. His ASCII-art graphics library became part of several other kids' games. And as a result, of course, he was extremely well respected by everyone, and a model for other kids' behavior.

When kids were possessive about their programs—and for a while there was a fad of building into game programs a list of who wasn't allowed to play them—I would remind them about all the people who contributed to their work, not only within the LS computer community but also, for example, Ken Thompson and Dennis Ritchie, who wrote the UNIX operating system we used, not to mention the taxpayers and the DEC stockholders who paid for the equipment. I didn't tell them what to do, but that doesn't mean I didn't express opinions about how fragile an idea intellectual property is.

It also helped when we started contributing to the Usenix software library. That meant that being communitarian rather than propertarian could get you known in the larger programming community—including, of course, Jay Fenlason's fame for writing *Hack*.

You remind me of my programming teacher in high school, who enforced a similar rule: we could make use of the computer lab as we saw fit, provided we turned in assignments and kept our grades up. Could you go into more detail on the rules and culture of the lab? The kids were allowed to come and go, day or night?

Officially, the kids were turned out by the security guard at 11:00 p.m. Once in a while a kid would hide when the guard came around, and I'd find the kid asleep on the couch in the morning. (This is one respect in which I really didn't understand that the life of a high school kid isn't like the life of an undergraduate for a reason. I'd pulled plenty of all-nighters in computer labs and thought nothing of it when a kid did the same at LS. Many years later I came to understand that that was a sign of something really wrong at the kid's home, calling for adult intervention.)

It helped that we were in a rich community, and it helped that there was no resale value for dumb terminals except to institutions. But even when we got a grant of Atari 800s to use as graphics terminals, none of them went missing. I was and remain very proud of that.

I had read A.S. Neill's *Summerhill* and was in love with the idea of kids making the rules. Our Computer Center Users' Society had weekly meetings that, like the Summerhill General Meeting, were both legislative and judicial. But (as Neill says in the book) it's hard to make self-government work in one classroom when the rest of the school is still adults governing the kids. Our kids weren't nearly as skilled as Summerhill kids at making the meetings work efficiently. Luckily, there were very few serious decisions to be made; the most contentious was who should take precedence when someone is playing games on a terminal and another kid needs it for schoolwork. This was settled with a computerized reservation system.

The kids also organized group social events. We had weekend picnics. The architecture of the room came up once in a while—for example, kids wanted coat hooks, even though of course every kid had a locker, because the lockers were far away from the computer center, and also the kids didn't trust their locked lockers as much as open coat hooks in the computer center.

Peter Blaser organized a chess club and got the school to pay for several plastic chess sets that could be taken out and played on our tables.

As for classes, I started out with an ambitious proposed sequence of courses, but ended up with only two: intro to computers and advanced computer programming. Intro had a sort of curriculum; there was a file cabinet with worksheets on various topics. Intro students had to do a minimal amount of Logo programming—just up to beginning recursion—and a minimal amount of word processing, so they could use the computers for their other schoolwork. After that they could do whatever they wanted, including playing computer games. I made game authors put their names and the school's name in the splash screen, so game players would think, *This was written by a kid just like me*, and be inspired to learn how.

I had gotten permission to offer classes pass/fail, and to pass intro, you had to do the minimal units and not much else. I also invented the variable-unit course, so a kid who took intro out of curiosity and turned out to hate it could complete and pass one unit, then quit, rather than failing two units. I never had as many curriculum worksheets as I wanted; I had hopes for much more than a kid could do in a semester, but as the community grew stronger, writing curriculum gradually felt less and less important to me. Instead what mattered was gathering tools: robot turtles, graphics terminals and printers, programming languages, a Usenet connection.

The kids who took advanced computer programming would start each semester with a proposal for what s/he (overwhelmingly he, alas) would accomplish that semester, and would get the credit for it at the end of the semester. Kids would take it repeatedly, I think less because they needed the units than as an excuse for the time they were spending in the computer lab.

You wrote about how the computer lab often look like... well, like a bunch of teenagers had the run of the place. Were you responsible for the lab's upkeep, or did the kids straighten up?

This is the story of how the Computer Center Users Society was born!

The school had custodians who cleaned the classrooms at night, but after a while they refused to work in the computer center because there was *so* much litter. For a while, when it got too terrible, one of us teachers would hit the stop button on the computer and make everyone clean up all the paper. But both the kids and the teachers hated this solution. Meanwhile, my other big pre-CCUS problem was that no matter how early I got to school, there'd be a dozen kids lined up outside the door waiting for me to let them in, and they would never let me go home at night.

It was Larry Davidson who had the brilliant idea of solving these two problems by combining them. Give kids keys to the room if they took on the obligation to keep the room clean. I immediately generalized that to the full *Summerhill* idea of putting kids in charge, period.

We were lucky in that the room had two doors. (This is a Massachusetts fire law for classrooms, but most rooms satisfy the law by having a door that connects to another classroom rather than to the corridor.) So we could leave the standard school lock that teachers have keys to in one of the doors, and put an entirely different lock in the other door.

I was hoping that CCUS members would choose to keep the room clean by cleaning up continually, so the room would always be clean, but instead they chose to set up a system in which one CCUS member each day, in rotation through the membership list, was in charge of cleanup at the end of each school day.

I liked your story about password hacking. Could you share others from the LS lab? What anecdotes have stuck with you?

Oh, lots. My favorite is about the time I needed some quiet time on the computer to solve a software problem, so I came in one Sunday at 10:00 a.m.—and couldn't get a terminal because they were all in use! But what makes this a funny story is that just as I walked in the door, one kid was saying to another kid, "I hate school." That was the only time I ever literally rolled on the floor laughing. (To which the kid said "This isn't school; this is the computer center.")

Another great moment won't seem so funny to you because it's one of those you-had-to-be-there stories, but I'll try: Kid A (male) and B (female) are sitting on the couch necking with great enthusiasm. Surrounding them are a cloud of other kids arguing vociferously about whether it's okay for A and B to behave that way in the computer center. Both sides of the argument had several adherents. I love those situations; the kids feel the weight of being in charge much more than when it's something obvious like cleanup.

Meanwhile, in the opposite corner of the room, C, who is the most clean-cut, proper, polite, dignified kid in the group, is teaching D, a freshman, how to play *Breakout*. Back at the argument, there's one of those moments when, for a second, nobody is talking. Just then, C says to D, "…and what you have to do is penetrate deeper." Everyone cracks up, and of course C makes it even funnier by saying "What? What'd I say?"

One time I pulled an all-nighter solving a system bug, and when kids started coming in in the morning, Jonathan [Payne] decided he was going to be me for the morning so I could rest. So the kids who would ordinarily have been calling "Brian! Brian!" to get me to come debug their programs were instead calling "Jonathan! Jonathan!" and at one point he did that cartoon thing of trying to walk in three directions at once. (Everyone got into this, and I think there were actually more requests for help than there would have been on a normal day.)

What can you tell me about Jay Fenlason, Kenny Woodland, Mike Thome, and Jonathan Payne? What grades were they in when you met, and what kind of students were they? Were they excited by the possibilities offered to them by computers?

That last question is funny; they all *lived* in the computer center. I don't really understand how any of the computer gang managed to pass their other classes. Most of them I met as freshmen, although some of them were still in junior high (this was before the invention of "middle school") when they started hanging out in the computer center after school hours.

[Digression for funny story. Every year the math teachers at LS had a joint meeting with the junior high math teachers to make sure they were all on the same page about what the high school teachers could expect kids to have learned in junior high. At one of these meetings, the teacher at Curtis Junior High who ran their school computer [lab] commented that kids didn't seem so interested in computers anymore; he used to have a bunch of kids hanging out after school but didn't any more. We had to explain to him where his kids were now.]

Jonathan was an exception. He spent his first two years hanging out at the library (and trying to get other kids in trouble by pulling the little magnetic strip off a library book and stashing it in someone's backpack). But we had terminals installed at the library, and you could play games on them, and—as I said earlier—the games made it clear that they were written by kids, and so late sophomore year he appeared in the computer center. But he very quickly became one of the leading experts; his big claim to fame was JOVE, an Emacs-subset editor for small computers.

Mike was much less bouncy than most of the kids. He liked to climb up to a little ledge at the top of one of the walls and sit there cross-legged reading. Don't misunderstand; he wasn't autistic or anything; he was very much part of the social group. He was just more able to sit in one place and not be in the heat of every ephemeral activity. So he became sort of the stereotype wise man of the group. Everyone looked up to him—me, too!—because he never yelled; he just always did the right thing calmly.

Jay, Mike, Jonathan, and Kenny created Hack in 1982 while at Lincoln-Sudbury. Did you follow Hack's development? If so, in what way? Did you encourage or contribute to it?
Really, Jay created *Hack*. Other kids contributed little bits. If you see names other than Jay's in the credits, it's because Jay really took in the lesson about not being possessive about one's creations. He did it because he wanted to improve Rogue, but—very unusually in those days—Rogue was distributed without source code.

I was certainly aware of *Hack*—I was their teacher, and I mostly knew about everyone's projects. I encouraged Jay as I encouraged everyone, but I didn't have any special feeling pro or con that particular project, if that's what you're asking. I'm sure Jay asked me questions as he was working, as everyone did, but I don't remember any particular way in which I contributed.

In my chat with Jay, he mentioned that you brought him and a bunch of other kids from LS out to California. Do you recall that trip?
That was my second time bringing LS kids to California for the summer. The first time was Peter Blaser, whom I came to know well during my first year at LS, when we still had the PDP-8. It had DECtapes for external storage, and kids wanted to be able to mount their own tapes to keep backup copies of their files, partly because the system crashed a lot. (We were running a third-party OS for the PDP-8 called ETOS, which the kids told me stands for "expensive ton of shit.")

But ETOS wouldn't let you use the DECtape drive unless you were an administrator (because it didn't have system calls to control it; the tape reading/writing program did direct hardware I/O). Peter had this complicated idea for how to let users run the DECtapes, basically by having a privileged daemon that would communicate with user programs via an ad hoc RPC mechanism he designed.

The previous generation of LS student sysadmins didn't think it would work, but Peter insisted that it would. Since debugging his idea would require standalone access to the PDP-8, it had to be done at night, after the other kids went home. Remember, this was long before we invented the CCUS. So I spent a lot of evenings in the computer center with Peter. Back in the '80s, people hadn't started worrying about teachers abusing kids sexually yet. (Of course I wouldn't be allowed to be alone with a kid so much today.) We were there quite late most evenings for a while—I'm not sure when he did his homework for the rest of school—so I took him out to dinner routinely. So, by the time summer came around, it just seemed really natural to take him out west with me. I've always been bicoastal since going to Stanford as a grad student, so it's common for me to spend summers on whichever coast I don't live on.

So that was a precedent. I think it was two years later that I was invited to do a summer workshop on Logo at SFSU—two workshops really, one for teachers and one for kids. I asked if I could bring kids along as teaching assistants, and ended up bringing Jay, Jonathan, and Robert. The latter two were already inseparable; it was during this summer trip that they became good friends with Jay. Besides the SFSU workshop we spent some time hanging around Stanford and Berkeley. (I guess it was at Berkeley that Jay discovered Rogue, right?) I ended up paying to replace some pillows in the SFSU dorm because of repeated enthusiastic pillow fights there.

So, anyway, the point of these trips wasn't especially educational, unless you count eating the world's best pot stickers at Hsi Nan. The point was just me sharing an adventure with my friends! But they did get to meet some of the heroes of computer science. Oh, and of course I took them to the Exploratorium—*that* was educational!

Could you tell me more about your involvement with the Logo programming language?
Logo predates my involvement by several years. I was introduced to it by Radia Perlman, who was then a grad student at the MIT Logo Lab. I started hanging out there mainly because I made friends with Henry and Julie Minsky, Marvin's kids, who hung out there a lot. But around the same time was when I started learning about progressive education—a housemate of mine left a copy of *Summerhill* lying around and I read it and was hooked. But I wasn't really involved in the actual work of the lab at that time. It was when I got to LS that I knew I wanted Logo as an environment for beginners, and there really wasn't one for UNIX. There was a sort of partial version of Logo controlling a robot turtle at, if my memory isn't failing me, the Ontario Science Center. I got their code and extended it into a full implementation of Logo.

Later, at Berkeley, I worked with several undergraduates to create the Berkeley Logo interpreter, which many people are still using. Dan Van Blerkom, who wrote the first implementation, had been a student of Molly Watt, one of the great Logo teachers, back in elementary school.

But really my biggest contribution to Logo, I think, was the _Computer Science Logo Style_ books. There have been about a bazillion books to introduce young kids to Logo, but from the beginning people at the MIT Logo Lab were saying that someone needed to write a more advanced book, because we knew that you could do much more with Logo than most people were doing. So finally I decided to do it, while I was working on my PhD at Berkeley, in between LS Logo and Berkeley Logo. The latter comes from my second stint at Berkeley, as a faculty member rather than as a grad student.

I started with the ambitious goal of introducing every subject in the CS curriculum, but eventually reduced my ambition to introducing only the topics I actually knew something (not very much) about: automata theory, discrete math, programming languages, and artificial intelligence. In each case I tried to make the text revolve around Logo programs that illustrate the ideas. (I'm not being modest about the "not very much"; pretty much everything I knew at the time is in those books, except that I couldn't figure out how to do operating systems in Logo.)

I had written a few magazine articles by then, and I figured that if an article takes me just a few days to write, and a book chapter is kind of like an article, I could easily dash off three volumes in less than a year. I was wrong; it was really hard. Each volume involved about eight months of spinning my wheels and hating myself, followed by three months of writing, and then a month of reformatting and doing the illustrations.

What led you to leave LS in 1982?

Ach—this is a hard question for me to answer. With the benefit of hindsight, I think the deep answer is that it was my first teaching job, I was very, very invested in it, I loved the kids, and therefore I took it personally when kids messed up. I wasn't yet a parent, and I guess I had an overly simplistic view about what teenagers are like, or what they could be like when put in charge of their own lives.

The surface answer is about password hacking. As I've written and you've read, the first time (that I know about) when a kid wanted to write a login simulator, I smiled benignly, thinking that that would be a minor activity. I myself grew up at the MIT AI Lab, where, back then, there was no such thing as passwords. I was certainly a hacker, in the original sense: I wanted to know how everything worked. But I had no curiosity about other people's secrets. So I under-estimated how much energy the LS kids would put into password hacking.

Over time I got more and more annoyed about it. At one point I modified our system so that turning off echoing required special privileges. And then finally, one day when I had the day off, I was called in because three kids had independently made efforts to crack the system and two of them had managed to break things to the point where nobody could log in. I was furious. (That evening my mom called me up, I said "*Hello?*" and she immediately said "What's the matter?" because she could hear it in my voice.)

That was, I think, in 1980–1981. And that's when I decided I was leaving. It took me another year to do it, because I had to hire and train my replacement. None of the candidates who applied had both the technical expertise and the progressive spirit we needed. In the end I twisted the arm of Paul Goldenberg, who'd been pivotal in getting me to LS in the first place, to take the job. But 1981–1982 was an unhappy time for me, and therefore for the kids too; I got angry a lot.

What led to you and the Hack crew staying in touch?

There's nothing special about *Hack* in this respect; I'm in touch with dozens of LS computer kids. This was probably the most intense time of my life. I felt part of a family, in a way I've never felt before or since. My best friends in the world are mostly LS teachers and kids. Former kids. Today is Jonathan's 50th birthday. Makes me feel antique. I'm even friends with some of the kids' kids!

Bonus Round: Work and @Play— An Interview with John Harris

Few gamers take on the audacious undertaking of tracing their favorite game genre back to its roots, documenting the decisions and trends that informed the development of each new entry along the way. John Harris is one exception to the rule.

Harris will be the first to admit that he isn't the best roguelike player, but it's very likely he is the most knowledgeable. In his long-running series, @Play, which ran on *Game Set Watch*, he dissected not only individual roguelike games, but their DNA—evaluating what decisions were made and why they did or didn't work.

His write-ups proved invaluable to me during research for *Dungeon Hacks*. After working my way through the entire catalog of @Play, I tracked Harris down and talked to him about his history with roguelikes, as well as the history of the genre in general.

*   *

What led to your interest in roguelike games, and the advent of your @Play column?
I had a cousin in Florida who had an old IBM PC compatible, one of the really early ones before the 286 [processor], running DOS. It ran on 5.25-inch floppies; it didn't even have a hard drive. He had a number of games he'd got from friends, and one was the widely pirated version of *PC Rogue*. I didn't know it was pirated at the time, but I played a great deal of that. That was the game that introduced me to it all. I'd never seen anything like it. For several years, that was the highlight of our visits to our cousins' place in Florida: booting up the computer, loading *Rogue*, and giving it a shot.

I thought it was amazing that the command file for *Rogue* was something like 15 kilobytes. It was an amazingly compact game. I played a great deal of it and came close to winning. *PC Rogue* was very difficult, even by roguelike standards. Since then, I've managed to win at *Rogue Clone*, which is closer to the UNIX version of *Rogue*, several times.

Later on, Game Set Watch put out a call for columnists on their site. I sent a message to Simon Carless, who thought @Play was a good idea. That's how that started.

I won't profess to be an expert on roguelikes, but it seems to me that the lack of modern graphics is the first hurdle new fans of the games have to jump. The depth of gameplay options and imagination involved in playing these games either captivates you and makes up for the lack of visual pizazz, or it doesn't. Would you agree?

Even at the time [I discovered *Rogue*], I had the impression that graphics weren't really required to make a game good. I'm old enough to remember the first video-game craze: the arcade boom of 1983. Back then, video games were primitive. The most popular game in the world for a while was *Space Invaders*, and that didn't have a color screen. But those were still interesting games. I played a lot of Infocom [adventure] games, and those didn't have graphics at all. So I never bought into the idea that games had to have good graphics to play well.

In fact, sometimes graphics can be a distraction. Good graphics can blind one to interesting types of gameplay.

The term "roguelike" has entered mainstream gaming's lexicon in recent years, mostly to describe a game as having roguelike mechanics such as permanent death and procedurally generated levels. What qualifiers do you feel a roguelike must exhibit to be considered a roguelike, rather than a game that happens to include roguelike mechanics?

The term "roguelike" has always been an ad hoc kind of thing; there's never been an official definition. It's a term people adopted to describe games like *Rogue*. *Rogue* came out, then *Moria* came along, and people said, "Okay, this game is like *Rogue*. We'll just call it a roguelike."

In a sense, it's something everyone decides for themselves. It's descriptive, not proscriptive. For me, for a game to be a roguelike, it has to be a game that takes the things that *Rogue* made interesting and uses them.

There are roguelikes I'm not too fond of. I've never really played *Angband*, but I still say it's a roguelike. I'm not sure it's useful to describe *Spelunky* as a roguelike, even though it incorporates a lot of the good ideas of roguelikes. It's a procedurally generated game, and so is *Rogue*. They both use similar ideas to similar ends, to produce entertaining experiences. Now, roguelike is used as a buzzword. You see half the new games released on Steam being compared to roguelikes.

I think, ultimately, these types of ideas are the future. A game is basically content that you churn through, and I think video and computer games are a much more profound thing than that. Exploring rules to produce very deep games that keep players interested for a very long time—that's really what *Rogue* is about. Exploring those rules through procedural generation, simple rules with profound consequences—all games [boil down to] that.

The European board-game boom that's going on right now follows that rule. *Settlers of Catan*, which is the most famous of the Euro games, has a randomly created board. Every time you play, you make the board out of these hexagons. You place numbered tokens, and the combination of those two procedures produces different gameplay each game. A lot of board games use randomization—in effect, a version of procedural generation that doesn't require a computer. You just follow the rules and you can create a new board with new gameplay implications.

Which of the mechanics invented or popularized by roguelikes is your favorite, if you could zero in on one in particular?

It's possible that procedural generation can turn out very flat and uninteresting. It's no mean feat to create a random dungeon, but that's not going to be interesting. A random layout of rooms and corridors isn't really that big of deal. It's just the same [collection of pieces], but the path is different each time. It's just a different way of presenting flat content.

[The focus should be] the content of the dungeon combined with random dungeon generation. So, you have a dungeon, right? And you have to explore it in order to find [the stairs leading down]. But there should be another function to exploration. Roguelikes do that through monsters and traps. They would just let you explore indefinitely. You can't just wander around willy nilly because you'll run out of food, or a trap will kill you, or, most likely, monsters will kill you.

You don't have an infinite amount of time to explore this space, and that's what makes the dungeon meaningful. If it was just a space you moved around in at no cost, it would not be interesting. But if there's some time limit, something that forces you to explore efficiently—that's interesting. Solving impromptu puzzles, figuring out the most efficient and safest way to explore a space, then that's interesting. Also, the items you find, the random resources with which to explore the space and overcome the dangers—all these systems working together are what make [roguelikes] interesting.

You've mentioned Angband as a roguelike you didn't care for; what features make you shy away from certain games?

I'm probably a minority in this: tactical combat adds a lot to roguelikes, but I think some games emphasize it too much. I never got into *Angband* because that game is mostly tactical combat. The aspects of roguelikes I enjoy the most, like random items and finding interesting uses [for them], are deprecated in *Angband*. I feel like they're almost put into *Angband* as lip service. But the thing is, the *Angband* model has expanded and become, basically, the massively multiplayer online game model.

Ultimately, *Angband* gave way to *Diablo*, and MMOGs all seem to follow the *Diablo* model. It's sort of the grind-and-mandatory-upgrade [formula]. Those are two things about role-playing games on computers that I'm not fond of. Grinding, especially, is the idea that you're playing a game and you have to pay your dues to the game before you get to the fun part. That can go away and die pretty quickly, I think.

In *D&D*, which is really the predecessor to all of this—*Rogue* wouldn't have existed without *Dungeons & Dragons*—a lot of *Rogue*'s systems can be traced back to *Dungeons & Dragons*. The aspects of *D&D* that *Rogue* took were deprecated in later editions. Things like item identification, strong resource management, and extremely deadly dungeon with more randomized components—things like that. Now, more recent versions of *D&D* work more like MMORPGs and [follow the] mandatory upgrade path.

This is something that became prevalent in Japanese RPGs: the idea that this town has the base equipment that you buy, so you go out and kill monsters for a while until you get the money for it. Then you buy it, and then you go to the next town. Now you have to buy the copper [equipment]. Then comes the iron stuff, then the steel stuff, then the Mithral stuff, then the diamond stuff, and the magic stuff—et cetera, et cetera. That stuff is just a mirror for your experience growth. They're two separate gameplay [components] that have the same function. There's no real reason to duplicate that.

The better [roguelike games] make you rely on what you find a lot more. You're not guaranteed to find the good stuff in order, or you might find the really good stuff early, or you might have to do without it because you never find it. Games like *Angband*, the way they [grade] the items that you find, you generally tend to find some items early and other items later on. It might almost be better if the game just automatically handed [certain items] to you when you reached a certain level. Just make that part of the experience progression.

So, grinding, and the idea of the mandatory upgrade path [are elements I could do without]. It's not hard and fast; you can have aspects of both that are important to the gameplay. I just think most games make too much of it.

What are some obstacles that you feel dissuade new players from catching on with roguelikes?

Part of it has to do with player pre-conceptions—about what games should be, and about what this kind of game [roguelike] should be. A lot of players come into roguelikes from other computer RPGs. Take a game like *Skyrim*—and I don't really need to pick on it; I like *Skyrim* a great deal—but the *Elder Scrolls* games in general, how enemies rise in power in parallel to you. It's this sense that a game is something you go through and win. You're bound to win. You *have* to win to complete the game. It's like a book that you go through to reach the end. When you're done with the book, it's over. I completed the book! I won the book! No.

[Players should not] think of a game as set content that they're bound to finish. Many times, a game designed like this will make [solving] the game easy so players can finish it. Shigeru Miyamoto, who I admire tremendously, puts secret paths to the end in *Mario* games. In *Super Mario Bros. 3*, there's the warp whistle; in *Super Mario World*, from World 2, you can get to the Star Road, and from the Star Road, you can get right to Bowser's back doorstep. So you can "finish" *Super Mario World* very quickly, really.

To appease those kinds of players, [taking shortcuts] is a much easier path than playing the full [game]. Then you've got Bowser at the end, and he's not a pushover, but you'll be able to beat him fairly easily compared to finishing some of the other levels in the game, which can be bastards. Every *Mario* game has a handful of levels that are, you know, *those* levels. But I think Miyamoto put in shortcuts to appease those players who won't be able to finish the game, or won't put the time or effort into it. I find it canny that he'd do that because, okay, you've beaten it, and now you can get down to the real point, which is finding every goal; that is the fun of any *Mario* game.

Players go into a roguelike with that expectation of, "Okay, this might offer 20 hours of gameplay. Let's start the clock!" Then they'll play, and they'll die, and they'll find out that they have to start over, and many of the things they learned before don't apply now because the dungeons are different; they might fight different monsters. That might put them off because they feel like they've lost progress.

I think it would help players new to roguelikes to think about the journey instead of the destination. In many roguelikes, you're never going to win. You need a graduate degree in *NetHack* to win *NetHack*. There are dozens and dozens of spoilers for *NetHack*. To really win, you're probably going to have to memorize three quarters of them. But if you look at it like that, you're never going to win, because you're going to look at it like a job.

Games aren't jobs. The way to enjoy roguelikes is to just play. If you enjoy it, fine. If not, maybe they're not for you. Once you get into them, though, there's so much there, and it's about the experience you have before you die. It's like, "Okay, this is going well. This is very

interesting—and I just died. But before I died, things were very interesting. I died in unex-
pected places." If you can get into that and think of roguelikes as random story generators,
where you're the protagonist of a story of your own making, that's awesome. I don't know of
any genre of game that does it better than roguelikes.

If you tell enough of those stories through playing and dying, eventually you learn the
things about the game that don't change every time. After enough of that, on some distant,
far-off day, you might actually win. Until that, you can have fun playing the way *you want to
play*, and use the high score list as a page in the book of your progress.

**I think that's what appeals to me about roguelike games. I'm terrible at them, but the sim-
plicity of their graphics and the idea that every adventure is different than the one before
stirs my imagination. I'm the captain of my ship and I'm setting sail for uncharted waters.**
That's why early *Dungeons & Dragons* was interesting. The early *Dungeons & Dragons* took
place as a single, huge dungeon that the dungeon master probably created himself on reams
of graph paper. Although the dungeon had set encounters, there was also leeway for lots of
randomness: random monsters, random items. Players cooperating in that environment tell
stories because they're characters in each other's stories.

That kind of play was very interesting—as opposed to the later forms of *Dungeons & Dragons*,
which were almost like fantasy novels. In fact, *Dragonlance*, that series of scenarios, basically
became fantasy novels. They sold pretty well at the time, but still, reading them, you could tell.

I think video games can be good storytelling tools, but shouldn't be restricted to that. The
games that play around with that are the most interesting. Games like *The Stanley Parable*. One
of the most popular of the Japanese RPGs, probably the best of the lot, is *Chrono Trigger*. You'll
never find any end of praise for it on the Internet, and the coolest thing about it is there are
all these different endings. In that way, you're exploring a story and adding elements of player
interaction.

**Hidetaka Miyazaki, director of Demon's Souls and Dark Souls, mentioned in an inter-
view that as a child, he attempted to read fantasy books written in English but struggled
to translate many of the words. He came to enjoy indecipherable passages because he
filled in blanks by making up translations, effectively taking control of the story for brief
periods of time. Do you think the proclivity of roguelike games to leave so much to the
player's imagination is responsible for the deep connection we feel to roguelikes?**
This goes back to player-driven storytelling, and people filling in the blanks. That's one thing
about graphics that does help out a lot: they tease blanks that you fill in. You could have the
Rogue gameplay in a [graphical] dungeon, but because the dungeon is more literal, it's more
obvious in that kind of environment that what you see the monster doing is what the monster
is doing. There's nothing else there.

Rogue leaves those spaces open. You don't know why *Rogue* monsters do the things they do.
If you find a scroll of monster detection, and if you read it and watch the monsters for a bit,
you'll see them doing things that make you say, "What are they doing that for?" Monsters will
run around in rooms, or a monster will walk up to a wall and just wait there. That lends an
imaginary life to the monsters, and [cause you to wonder] what they do when the player isn't
around.

I think that's very important to this kind of game. In a way, it's the designer's best friend. There's a role-playing game rulebook, *Call of Cthulu*, one of my favorite games and an extremely well-written book. Sandy Petersen and Lynn Willis were the authors. There's a chapter about getting new keepers, a new game master for the game. This is a quote: "When the keeper sets a scene, his or her most important ally is [the player's imagination]. Reasonable deduction consists of all which is in the room, or cabin, or aircraft, or other visible setting, which is not described as being there, but can be logically inferred as being there."

The book talks about, if you're in a study, that means there's probably a light source, windows, books, bookshelves, there might be a desk and a lamp on the desk, and a bottle of brandy on the desk. All of these things have potential uses in the game. In computer games, those things really don't exist, but you can imagine them. They're not visibly there; there's no human running the game; there's a computer. But you can still imagine them as window dressing.

That is the source of people imparting a life unto monsters, or imagining the story of why their avatar is in the dungeon, or imagining malice on part of the dungeon itself. Although it's not important to the game, some of the most fun you can have with roguelikes actually doesn't involve playing them, but involves going into the Usenet groups and reading players' stories about their games.

I devoted two or three columns in @Play to that. One player started playing a character whose ambition in life was to be a dragon. She found the ring of polymorph and an amulet of polymorph control. She slips on the ring, drinks the potion of polymorph, specifies "black dragon," then slips on the amulet. Dragons have lots of disadvantages, but she went on to win the game anyway.

Those make for interesting reading even if you don't know a lot about the game. I think those are important and can be a big part of the game.

A high bar of difficulty seems to be par for the course in most roguelikes, executed through systems such as permanent death and cursed items. Do you think difficulty constitutes an important component in the roguelike formula?

The classic style of roguelike play, dating back to *Rogue* itself, and beyond it to classic First Edition [1E] *D&D* and Original *D&D*, presents the dungeon as a towering challenge to be overcome. The harder the dungeon, the greater the sense of accomplishment when it's beaten. However, most characters die, so a high score list provides a sense of progression and accomplishment to keep players involved until then, and to satisfy players who may never reach it.

Much as it was in arcades, this style of play is helped by a social environment, whether it be a darkened arcade, a college computer lab, a UseNet group, a website like alt.org, or a circle of roguelike-playing friends, as it was with me. People to compete against, to cheer on, to commiserate with.

Some roguelikes place heavy emphasis on identifying items carefully, through scrolls rather than experimentation. Others feel identifying gets in the way. Where do you stand on the issue? How important is identifying items to roguelike DNA?

I think it's not necessarily essential, but it can add a tremendous amount to the game, if the system is designed correctly. Item identification is something that was a big part of classic *D&D* but has fallen away from more recent editions of that game.

As a general rule, how do you feel about roguelikes that throw out cleared levels and generate new ones when players backtrack, versus keeping old levels?

It varies. Generally I think it's better to retain levels, both because it makes the dungeon feel more like a real place and because it means players can't "scum" for items by re-exploring the same level repeatedly.

But it depends on the rest of the design. Since *Angband* pretty much requires players to have certain stats by certain levels, if players couldn't farm stat gaining items, there would be a strong chance players would be unprepared by the time he gets [to later levels]. That would mean the game would have to lessen that aspect of the difficulty to remain fair.

How do you keep the procedural generation of roguelikes from stepping over the line that separates difficult and cheap? Should every level be winnable, or is it okay to present an insurmountable challenge?

The game has to be winnable, if the goal is to win, full stop. Designers should think carefully about this. That said, it doesn't have to be *easy* to win. It is acceptable to provide very difficult, yet still possible, ways to progress if the easier levels were not [procedurally] generated. *NetHack* might be a bit too easy to win in this regard, provided the player is perfectly spoiled; if he is not, *NetHack* remains extremely challenging.

In @Play, you've held up *Rogue* as one of your favorite roguelikes. How do you think *Rogue* has held up in the decades since it began spreading across computer networks?

I think *Rogue* is still a fine game. I think [good] game design doesn't go obsolete. If you have a really good game, then it's a good game because of what people think of it. It will eventually find an audience if it doesn't find one at first. It had an audience at one point and could one day find one again. There are games that are popular for fad-ish reasons: because it's new, or they've never seen something like it before. But then, after a while, the luster wears off.

Rogue is not a game like that. *Rogue* is playable now. It's still as challenging as it was before, and it wouldn't have been as hyper-popular as it was back then if that wasn't the case. You don't hear as much about it, but in some ways, *Rogue* is still the best roguelike because its different systems fit together the best. It's a game designed in such a way that you can't rely on any one thing. You can find an item that puts one part of the game completely out of play. You can find a ring of low digestion, and food never becomes a factor. But you do want to put on other rings. No one item will make *Rogue* an instant win because almost all of the items are random.

**
Rogue set a precedent of confining dungeons to a single screen. Games derived from *Rogue*, such as *Hack* and *NetHack*, carried on that tradition, whereas *Moria* and its ilk spread dungeons across several screens. Do you think *Rogue*'s single-screen dungeon hurt its scope?**

There are few games that turn out better than *Rogue* has. People have made *Rogue* with larger dungeons. In one of my articles, I mentioned the *Rogue* restoration project. A lot of people made games like Super *Rogue* and *Ultra Rogue* that are practically forgotten these days. They only existed to form the binary for long-vanished operating systems, things that hadn't run for decades except maybe through emulation.

Rogue's design is strongly tied to the size of game it is. The game is just long enough that you have a pretty good chance of finding many items that are useful, but no guarantee. You probably won't see half the rings [available] in one game. I think that's good because it forces you to play different ways each time. If you made *Rogue* larger without changing that, you'd have to make the items rarer. If you make the items rarer, the game wouldn't be as exciting because you wouldn't find cool stuff as frequently.

To make *Rogue* a lot more interesting if you wanted to make it larger, you'd have to make more items, which is difficult to do, in a way that maintains a consistent quality [of items]. It would be exponentially more work, the larger you made *Rogue*. I think *Rogue* is the perfect size for what it is, but other games have their own items, so it's different for them.

NetHack feels a little too large, but I think it holds together well. *NetHack* is difficult to talk about because there are so many great things and weird things about it.

Angband requires players to boost over a dozen resistances, as well as understand level-generation algorithms, tactics, items, and more. Similarly, as you've mentioned, many players believe the best way to approach *NetHack* is to read spoilers so you know more or less what to expect from the toughest levels. When does a roguelike demand too much?
It's a sliding scale. I think the tracking down of resistances is generally an over-valued aspect of roguelike design. It's something that a number of classic roguelikes do. If a game requires that a player have some specific attribute to get past a certain point, then to be fair, the game has to have some way of gaining that infallibly by that point, or somehow allow the player to keep generating items until it can be gained before that point, in order to ensure the game is winnable. I generally think most classic roguelikes—but not *Rogue*—go a bit too far in this direction.

Do you think roguelikes in general, rather than elements of roguelikes that find their way into games like *Diablo* and *Chocobo Dungeon*, can be mainstream? Do they need to be?
They can be, and have slowly been moving in that direction. I think ultimately the basic "dungeon exploration game" without enlivening elements, like challenging opponents, randomization, strong resource management, identification, and other non-combat challenges, is basically a dead-end. It is telling that roguelikes provide so many of the solutions to making dungeon exploration interesting, possibly, because it got many of them from classic *D&D*.

Index

Page numbers in *italic* indicate figures and page numbers followed by n indicate notes.

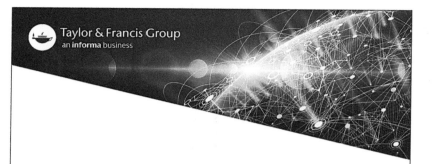